· CIRCLE OF STONES SERIES ·

JUDITH DUERK

Volume I— Circle of Stones: Woman's Journey to Herself
Volume II— I Sit Listening to the Wind: Woman's Encounter within Herself

I SIT LISTENING TO THE WIND

· CIRCLE ºF STONES SERIES ·

JUDITH DUERK

I SIT
LISTENING
TO THE WIND

Woman's Encounter Within Herself

San Diego, California

LuraMedia™

Copyright © 1993 by LuraMedia
San Diego, California
International Copyright Secured
Publisher's Catalog Number LM-642
Printed and Bound in the United States of America

Cover design by Nelson Kane
Cover woodcut by David Klein

LuraMedia
7060 Miramar Road, Suite 104
San Diego, CA 92121

Library of Congress Cataloging-in-Publication Data
Duerk, Judith.
I sit listening to the wind : woman's encounter within herself /
by Judith Duerk.
p.   cm. — (Circle of stones series ; v. 2)
ISBN 0-931055-98-9
1. Women—Psychology. 2. Femininity (Psychology).
3. Identity (Psychology). 4. Sex role. I. Title.
II. Series: Duerk, Judith. Circle of stones series ; v. 2.
HQ1206.D86   1993
155.3′33—dc20   93-991
                                        CIP

to
the memory
of a woman
who struggled
to
bring forth
herself

Acknowledgements

My thanks to the women who have allowed the use of their dreams and writings and to the circles of women everywhere who have given loving encouragement as this book progressed.

My acknowledgement to LuraMedia and to the courage and risk-taking of Lura Geiger and Marcia Broucek in dealing with a complex and difficult subject.

My gratitude to Bobbi Kadesch for her help in preparing the manuscript and for her good humour and patience in all stages of the work.

And lastly, my heartfelt appreciation to my husband, my two sons, and my brother for support during the entire effort. This writing could not have been brought to completion without the real and honest support from both the Feminine and Masculine realms.

CONTENTS

How might your life have been different if, once, as a young girl... when you wandered alone in the woodlands not far from your mother's house... you had come upon a small glade you had never seen before?

If, as you listened to the wind blow mysteriously... you had seen, there in the shadows, a circle of rough-hewn stones? And, as soon as you saw the stones, you sensed the wisdom waiting there... knew that this was a place where women had gathered throughout the ages to reflect upon their lives.

And you sat down quietly on one of the stones... as if the stones, themselves, would teach you what you needed to know.

How might your life be different?

I sit listening, the wind blows . . . an image comes to me . . . of a woman in a moment of reflection . . . sitting quietly to listen within.

She listens to her own Feminine feelings and perceptions, but also to her inner Masculine side.

Then, in her own individual way, she enters a life-long encounter as she engages with this Masculine energy, which spiritual traditions throughout the ages have characterized as "the Wind." It is the Masculine/Yang energy within a woman's Feminine/Yin psyche. It brings her balance and strength and completes her wholeness as a woman.

Jung called this Masculine energy the "animus."

I have used these terms interchangeably in this writing:

woman/Yin/Feminine   man/Yang/Masculine

animus/woman's Masculine side/
the Masculine energy within the Feminine psyche

Preface

The years spent working with this material have been among the most difficult of my life.

Even as I write these words, I am aware of a voice saying, "This book is neither definitive nor authoritative. It is too subjective to be of consequence. Mostly," says the voice, "everyone knows all of this already."

"And besides, it's a trifle boring!"

I smile. How like that voice within a woman, as it dismisses her, to end with a little swipe: "and haven't you put on a bit of weight?"

This writing was begun to explore the dismissing voices of the Masculine side of a woman as she struggles to listen within and to bring forth her own perceptions. *And, even as I write of the dismissing voices, a voice dismisses me.*

Writing of woman's Masculine side has been a very different experience from writing of the Feminine realm. My animus began with such wit and verve that it took me several chapters to realize that I had been tricked: He wanted to make this book a compendium about himself, quite unrelated to woman's life and needs.

There is an old idea that to speak directly of an Archetype brings it to life right there in the room. And it proved disturbingly true! As I tried to write, the animus protested . . . did not want to be revealed as he really was . . . but capered around the room, distracting me in a dozen directions . . . crept in, wordy and pompous, with grandiose proclamations. Strife erupted in our household between me and my husband, my sons. I remembered how the animus can make mischief between a woman and the men around her, but I wasn't quite prepared for all of this!

I knew that I must renew my grounding in the Feminine realm. I spent many days in the woods, simply picking up sticks . . . remembering how deeply I cared for the women for whom I was preparing this writing and how devoted I felt to the Feminine process of us all.

I felt the pathos of women today with our overdeveloped animus, confronted with the eternal paradox: The nature of the Yin is receptive, to yield . . . the nature of the Yang is to dominate. The two are forever equal and necessary to the fulfillment of the cosmic cycle. We modern women, with our powerfully developed inner Masculine side, are faced with a new dilemma: whether to ground ourselves in the vibrant receptivity of the Yin, or to give over to our dynamic and compelling animus mode.

Until a woman consciously engages with the Masculine energy within, she remains under its domination. She does not emerge as an individual . . . but espouses the common patterns and practices of the society around her. She is cut off from her womanly subjectivity, risks losing the underlying guidance of the Self.

Especially if a woman lacks experience or conviction in the steadfastness and self-restraint required to remain centered in the Yin, she may abdicate completely to an animus mode. She totally loses her footing in the Feminine ground and her connection through it to the deeper Self. She accommodates to a group ethos.

I see a broader pattern in our country that parallels this, in which people go to extreme measure to accommodate to the group, leaving behind any individual connection to the deeper Self. Surely this pattern needs to be broken, particularly in these critical times when the deepest possible wisdom is needed!

In her efforts to effect change in our society, modern woman may not realize that she leaves unexplored Feminine modes that might accomplish the same ends if she could rediscover them . . . modes of holding within herself her vision of what could be . . . of gestating that vision with a spiritual energy that is uniquely Feminine . . . and finally, bringing it forth in a circumspect womanly voice.

Perhaps modern woman has no idea how profoundly she is needed. The world is crying out for a developed Feminine voice, a voice that can mediate, once again, the ancient values of the Feminine . . . values of interiority, of the sacredness of matter . . . values that honour the privacy of individual process.

There is a story of canaries, valued for their sensitivities, that were taken below the surface in old mines to test for poison gas. Women, today, frequently express impatience with themselves for being "overly sensitive." Yet, I sense that our culture is in desperate need of women of sensitivity and courage who can point out what is poisonous just below the surface . . . women who have grounded themselves, developed their vision and voice, and can identify what is twisted in our society today.

In my writing, I speak often of daughters, but I do not mean biological daughters. I am fiercely proud of my sons and of their spiritual energy. Yet, I recognize a distinctly Feminine spiritual energy . . . an energy that flows from the Archetypal Great Mother herself. I ask myself how we women today can open ourselves to this ancient flow? . . . let it flow through us to our daughters, to the women of the future, to the daughters of all of us?

How can we rediscover old modes of remaining centered within and rooted in the deeper Self? Explore the possibilities of these modes and offer them to the society around us?

How can we modern women work with the cooperation of our animus, not under its domination? Ask its aid in bringing forth, again, the true values of the Archetypal Feminine . . . and of the Self within us all?

An ancient Oriental image reveals beautifully the relationship of the mature woman with her developed animus: It is the lingam in the yoni, the phallus embraced in the vulva. The image symbolizes the Masculine energy within a woman's psyche offering itself in devoted and loving penetration . . . offering its energy in willing commitment to the woman, as she, with her roots in the ground of the Yin, brings forth the flowering of the Feminine Self.

I offer this book not as an encyclopedia about the animus, but as a helpful companion to sustain a woman as she begins her encounter within.

I sit listening to the wind . . . as woman has listened so long . . . in wonder at its energy and what it stirs within her . . . seeking to hold her ground and not be blown away. Sensing, with an ancient sense, the work that is hers to do to develop herself and her gifts as she engages with the Masculine energy within her Feminine psyche . . . the small Yang circle of light within her soft Yin darkness.

Great cycles of a woman's life . . . early bonding with the mother . . . through that bond, a grounding in the Archetypal Feminine . . . underneath that, roots in the deeper Self. The awakening of her Masculine side and a loosening of those earlier bonds . . . schooling and professional life, fulfilling her achievement side . . . perhaps marriage and children. Years of satisfying her obligations in the collective realm surrounding her.

For modern woman there follows a period of great possibility, of conscious work with her Masculine energy, asking its help to focus on Archetypal Feminine values and to assist her in bringing those values to manifest form in her life. And in a woman's later years, the journey back to Feminine ground . . . her devotion in that realm, as she brings forth her truest voice.

In a complete absence of animus energy, there is no life, the air is dead. A woman is unable to develop, without clarity or focus. But for many modern women, that Masculine energy is ever there, ever blowing, filling any vacuum left when she fails to know her feelings or define her values . . . filling the void with judgements and criticisms repeated from the society around her, with little regard for the woman's own subjective truth or wisdom.

Until a woman recognizes and engages with her inner Masculine side, it operates autonomously. She may not even be able to see that something is out of control. She will have to address this Masculine side of herself and form a relationship with it. Until she accomplishes this, her womanly energy is spent in service to the collective realm and to its competitive system. And her woman life is lost!

The following story illustrates a modern woman's dilemma:

Already a physician in her own country, a woman had earned two doctoral degrees in America before returning abroad for training as a psychoanalyst. In the early stages of that work, she remarked to her professor, a man of compassion and honesty, that she feared she might have too much ego to submit willingly to the work. His reply was that she had "very little Feminine ego at all, only a highly trained animus."

Thus begins the story of modern woman's encounter within.

HER GROUNDING
IN THE
FEMININE

A sense of time

I sit listening to the wind . . .
        . . . the woods are cool and quiet.

The wind blows . . . brings a memory from many years ago:

The storms of early autumn had felled large trees and branches in the woods nearby. For several days the men had worked to clear away the timber. The firewood had been cut in lengths and neatly stacked to dry. What was left was in a heap of brush and twigs. It was an eyesore, in the way, and in the very place I had wanted to write for the next few days.

There was no one else to clean it up, so I started with a vengeance, intending to make short shrift of it and get on with my real work. For a few hours I laboured furiously, pulling at the pile, grabbing at the ends of the largest branches, trying to disentangle the heap by sheer brute force and my accumulated animosity. I learned later that a young woodsman had returned, willing to work, but had fled in fright before the ferocity of my face and efforts.

By late morning, it was clear that nothing effective was happening. My petulant tearings and rippings at the pile finally began to slow down. Much of my irritation had worn itself off . . . the woods had worked its way.

I stopped to sit on a nearby rock and knew that I must eat.

When I went back to work, it was with a different energy . . . no longer impatiently pulling at the protruding limbs or trying to overturn the heap. With clippers, I began to trim whatever offered itself from the stack. In my agitation of the morning, I had not seen that it could be approached in this way.

By late in the afternoon, I knew there was no way that the task would be finished that day. I began to work more slowly, to sink into my experience with the brush. To the right went branches, neatly stacked, ready for drying or burning. To the left I placed little bundles of twigs to be used later as kindling.

As the shadows lengthened, a quieter rhythm emerged. The task seemed more worthy of itself . . . my real work, less pressing. I stopped before I grew too tired and, much to my surprise, began to write, as I had first intended, right there beside the brush.

On the morning of the second day, I awakened early with a sense of eagerness, not to finish the job of clearing, but to see what the day might bring if I offered myself to the task. At intervals I rested, with no clear plan for what must be completed that day. It was almost no surprise to find myself writing in the woods as I rested.

The day passed.

Near the middle of the third day, I became aware of something wondrous happening. My whole experience was shifting . . . the molecules of time, itself, opened up before me . . . spreading themselves apart so that there was space and breadth amongst them . . . breath to breathe within each moment.

I laid down the clippers and sat on the rock to sense the moment more fully, as I had not allowed myself to do the day before.

I saw the wind in the tallest trees slowly stir the leaves. The colours shifted from darkest greens to black . . . to nearly yellow. A hush was in the woods around, as well as deep within, me. I watched there, while the sun set, then walked silently to the house.

I washed my hair and did the few things necessary to prepare for the coming week.

The next morning, as the fourth day dawned, the whole house lay in quietness. The preparations of the evening before, undertaken out of silence, had emerged from a sense of ordering far deeper than conscious planning. What had not been done never would be missed.

When I returned to the woods to work, I carried a broom with the clippers. By noontime, all of the remaining twigs had been put into the little bundles and tied with yarn from the house, for there was no twine. I swept the ground where the brush had been, smoothing out the last bits of bark. The earth lay flat and clean again . . . the grass, a pale yellow.

The wind blows . . . I sit leaning against a tree.

Many times, through the years, I have remembered that fourth day. There was a sense of being deep within the doing. Rather than a driven way of pressing to complete the task, knowing every second what the next ten thousand would hold, it was as if I had slipped through a scrim into a timeless, mysterious realm . . . silent . . . shimmering with life.

One whole day of being, not in ordinary Chronos time, but in the sacred Kairos time of the Feminine realm. I had glimpsed a way of being in which time, itself, was sentient, quivering with its own awareness of what each moment could hold.

A way of being . . . from long ago . . . when the earth was still held sacred. When a woman knew that her task was necessary to the cycles of nature . . . knew that her devotion within, as she fulfilled the task, reconsecrated the earth and echoed throughout the cosmos.

The locust tree at my back sways. I think of our needs as women. Our ordinary lives are no longer lived in nature. It is difficult, in daily life, to find the Feminine realm. The drawing of the water, the gathering of the grains no longer are performed under an open sky. Even the machines that assist a woman prevent her from holding the elemental in her hands. The sense of her task as consecrated and necessary to the cosmos is gone.

Under the pressures of modern life, time has become compressed. The sense of sacred Kairos time has all but disappeared. Yet woman cannot exist with only a linear awareness of time. There must be time enough for her to experience the sacredness within the moment and within herself.

How can woman redeem what was lost so long ago? For millennia, as she was defined by man, woman developed herself in the prevailing Masculine image. But the heroic journey of the Masculine, so long clearly delineated, could not provide what was needed to complete the journey of the conscious and developed Feminine . . . It could not help woman return to her Archetypal roots or to the sacredness of her sense of Kairos time.

I sit listening to the wind and think of our task as women ... of the past, how far our grandmothers came ... of the future, open before us. What will our generation of women pass on to our daughters? What will be our legacy to the daughters of our great-grand-daughters?

What will help us learn once more
how to let the moment slip
as if slipping
through
an eternal
glass
from the purposeful
and known

... to the timeless?

How might your life have been different if, once when you were young, struggling to fulfill what you thought ought to be done, but afraid that there would never be time enough for you . . . something had quietly drawn you to go for a walk in the woods? If you had slowly walked away from the noise crowding in on you . . . until you heard, from within yourself, a silence you had almost forgotten?

If, as you watched the dappled shadows on the ground around you, the wind had suddenly stilled . . . and there was a silence so profound that you entered a new sense of time . . . of time stretching out before you? And you knew that there would be time enough to let your whole life emerge.

How might your life be different?

A sense of identity

I sit listening . . .
. . . the wind blows.

An old woman sits with me . . . watches as the aspen leaves flutter to the ground. She speaks of her struggle of the past:

"It was not like it is now. There was no way a woman could succeed but to give up parts of herself. We entered, all alone, into the unknown . . . with little to support or sustain us from a familiar realm.

"I was one of the few women teaching at the conservatory when an announcement was made that a master class was to be presented by a woman of great renown. There were stories of her superb artistry, as well as of her imprisonment and narrow escape in the war. Her concert the evening before the class had brought tumultuous applause.

"I wondered at her appearance the next morning, as she walked across the stage. She carried a brown leather satchel, worn-looking, with a frayed handle . . . settled her materials on a small table, rather than on the imposing podium alongside. One could see her frailness. Yet her presence filled the hall in a way I had not seen before.

"She requested a glass of water and asked to be certain that the members of the audience, waiting with some impatience, were comfortable. The last thing she did before she began the class was to cross over to where her brown satchel sat on the floor and to take out of it a faded, rose-coloured sweater,

8

which she put on over her fashionable gown. There was a small hole at the left elbow.

"She said the hall felt a little drafty.

"The audience, candidates for graduate diplomas, had arrived well before she came. There were faculty and dignitaries from two hundred miles around sprinkled throughout the auditorium. The woman was to coach a handful of performers pre-selected by a panel. The class began quietly. The woman tried to put the young musicians at ease. She spoke of submitting one's skill and mastery to bring forth the pathos and meaning from the heart of the music itself."

The old woman sighs, then continues:

"It was what happened at the close of the day that has lingered with me so long. In the customary question period, the students and scholars seemed caught up in outdoing one another, as sometimes happens on those occasions. Several extremely technical questions were asked and thoroughly answered. Then, as if a fever fell over the auditorium, the questions became abstract and belaboured.

"In her quiet way, the woman artist began to turn away the questions. 'No,' she said to this one, 'that issue denies the spirit of the day.' 'No,' to another, she did not feel qualified to answer in that area, 'but perhaps,' she wondered, 'might there be someone in the auditorium who does?' After several more questions had been turned away, the woman expressed concern that the soul of the music was being lost.

"There was a rustle of unrest. The question period abruptly ended. The dean of the conservatory thanked the woman artist and brought the master class to a close. As the audience emptied down the center aisle and out the rear door, the

woman crossed over again to where the worn, brown satchel sat on the floor and folded her sweater into it.

"Several of the young women performers lingered on the stage . . . tried to engage the woman, again, in questions. She answered only one, with the simplest and briefest of answers. She started to say that she was tired, but the questioners had already left, in haste and disappointment.

"I saw that two more young women still waited in the shadows. One asked if she might help the woman artist with the satchel. She responded with thanks, asked if they would join her for a cup of tea . . . it would be nice to have companionship while she waited for her train."

The wind blows. Leaves fall more quickly around us as the old woman speaks:

"I have wondered, all these years, at the presence that woman had, there at the close of the day. She knew so truly who she was, knew the value of what she gave . . . Did not press herself to give more. My own tendency would have been quite different . . . young, then, as I was, and eager for success.

"All day, before an erudite audience, she had offered her consummate artistry, given of her generativity to inspire the younger musicians. As the late afternoon had faded into evening, she entered another realm.

"That one moment influenced profoundly my whole life as woman. I felt the ground underneath me shift . . . sensed, for the very first time, that other realm a woman might choose in which to live her life . . . a different mode to bring her meaning beyond goal-directed accomplishment."

The old woman reaches out her hand . . . catches a leaf as it falls:

"All these years, I have wondered, what became of those young women . . . the first few, so disappointed that the woman artist refused to be other than she was. And the courage of those last two who remained . . . while all the others left!

"I have wondered if they could see, already at their age, the choices she had made? . . . her brilliant development in the Yang realm . . . and her grounded return to the Yin? I hoped her intelligence and grace, as she fulfilled her task, helped those young women strike their own roots in that other ground."

I sit listening to the wind, in wonder at its power to freshen or devastate . . . in wonder, also, at the Masculine energy within a woman that can enliven her development or completely dominate it . . . that can allow her to bring forth her gifts or keep her from ever knowing who she truly is.

The wind blows
    . . . blows.
        Leaves fall.

How might your life have been different if, as a young woman, struggling to find out who you were, you had known of a special place that could help you ground yourself? And you had pulled your warmest sweater from the hook beside the door . . . and had set off, all alone.

And, as you walked in the gathering dusk down the loneliest part of your path, you drew the sweater more closely around you . . . until, finally, you entered that special place and stood quietly breathing in the stillness. And the silence and the darkness helped you be present to yourself.

How might your life be different?

A sense of sustenance

The wind blows...
        ...chill and wild.

I put a log on the fire, glad to be warm and safe, thankful for this time of quiet to reconnect with myself.

I remember sitting quietly one winter, long ago. My children were very young then... slept peacefully in the next room. I read, one evening, of an experiment that left a deep impression on me, of baby monkeys given a choice between a wire or soft mother. The wire figure had a mechanical apparatus that dispensed a feeding... the soft form, only a cushioned lap and pillowed body to lean against. The babies who survived best were those who chose the soft mother.

I wondered, alone there, that night, if my children would know to choose the soft mother in their lives. Had they received enough nurture to know what would sustain them?... enough elemental holding and touching to know how to care for their lives? And now, as I sit in the stillness and think of the lives of women today, of the myriad choices open to us, I wonder if we know to choose what truly will sustain us.

The wind blows an icy blast... drives sleet against the window.

I shiver as I consider the changes in the last few generations. Our grandmothers did not have the opportunities open to us now. There was little conscious understanding of the Archetypal Feminine. Women undervalued themselves and the nurturing roles they filled . . . only the wire mother was known.

Four women speak of the meaning of their ordinary lives. The first woman speaks of her struggle to ground her life:

"I am so confused as I try to sort things out. My mother taught her three daughters her own most important rules: Keep all options open. Make only goal-directed choices. Hold to universal ideals.

"As long as I work extended hours, have no time to reflect or feel, I can endure my life. After all, I tell myself, I've more than fulfilled Mother's aspirations.

"But when I overhear other women talking about their lives, I feel scared and hollow. They seem to settle into their lives in a way I've never allowed myself . . . struggling to keep all my options open.

"I feel a longing for a woman's life I have never known, that my mother never knew, either. In my very worst moments, I grasp frantically at all my citations and awards, trying to draw comfort from somewhere, from anywhere, at all."

The second woman speaks:

"I went to my mother and sister, troubled about my life and marriage, hoping to be listened to and received by woman's ears. But they couldn't hear my pain as I struggled to ground my life on something more substantial than my old self-image from the past.

"Everything then had been only a reflection of my surroundings, chosen from the pages of popular women's magazines . . . my hair style and wardrobe, our home and furnishings, even the company we kept. Nothing reflected me.

"I had been offered a position of power and prestige, and I feared that my family wanted me to accept it. I would have to be away, leave the care of our home to strangers . . . abandon the intimacy of our lives. An old, Masculine voice inside me said that it was important to move ahead. I knew I had to sort out where that voice came from or I would think that it was my husband's.

"If only I could tell him how much my mornings meant to me . . . the special quality of quietness
 in the empty, dark kitchen . . .
  . . . soft flutter of wings at the feeder
   . . . the rustle of pages in my journal.

"My mother and sister just kept saying, 'What is the matter with you?' Mother, especially, was adamant: 'You've always tried to get by! If you don't take this job, you'll hold the family back!'

"I escaped from the encounter wounded, but alive, feeling a terrible failure. An image came to me of a river flowing with life but overlaid with a metallic matrix that kept everyone from its waters . . . like my mother's calendar, full of scheduled events and pre-planned social affairs . . . but offering no real sustenance.

"I realized how barren the lives of my mother and sister were. And I felt a sudden stab of compassion for our whole Feminine process . . . my mother, unable to acknowledge my pain because her own had never been acknowledged . . . my sister and I, never helped to embrace ourselves or our ordinary lives.

"When my needs became clear to me, I was able to say them so that my husband could hear me."

The third woman, somewhat older, listens and then begins to speak:

"I think I always chose the wire mother in my life, pushed myself in a very driven way. In my dreams I was employed by the U.S. Department of Labor: work to gain ambition and glory rather than to sustain the basic stuff of life. I could never play or rest, and I distrusted any woman who did.

"I remember the women's gatherings I attended so many years ago. If they were not directed from an intellectual point of view, I was impatient and ill at ease, awkward with the women and hating all the silence.

"I wanted so badly to change that unrelenting side of myself . . . I knew that I could no longer live by those old 'ideals.' And things are finally changing. In a lovely series of recent dreams, I am working in children's theatre. And a radiant young woman, who could be a Goddess, joyfully welcomes me into a circle of women. I am finding a way to belong among women . . . a way of belonging in my life."

The oldest woman reflects on her experience in a group of women:

"All employed in demanding positions, we gathered every month. Time after time we resisted the plea of the woman who led the group to turn aside from our restless search and to look within ourselves. She spoke earnestly at the end of a day, imploring us to leave behind lofty, spiritual quotations and to simply share the experiences of our ordinary lives.

"The group regathered the next month. It was the time of the winter solstice . . . the darkest days of the year. Two of the women had been ill, and the energy of all of us was at an ebb.

"As we entered the space she had prepared for us, our customary silence deepened. The light from the windows was already dim . . . the darkness worked its way. In the half-light from the candles and the fire on the hearth, we left our intellectual mode . . . entered a quieter, darker place within ourselves we had not known was there.

"One woman after another, we shared our struggle against emptiness, our need to keep busy to avoid despair. We shared our anguish with one another, our longing for a way of life that could more deeply sustain us.

> *"The grey light at the windows grew fainter,*
> *. . . the room became hushed and still.*
> *As the candles burned low,*
> *one woman sang a lullaby.*

"The wind hummed low in the chimney."

How might your life have been different if there had been a place for you to go when your life was difficult and you felt utterly alone ... a place of safety and comfort?

If a woman whom you trusted had been there to receive you ... had listened silently, as you spoke your discouragement? And then she had covered you warmly as you curled up for a rest.

And, if she briefly went out ... and returned with an armload of wood ... and quietly built up the fire and sat down nearby to tend it ...

How might your life be different?

A sense of voice

Late winter . . .
. . . the wind blows.

An image from a woman's dream drifts through the cold to me:

"A beautiful young woman stands on a snowy field. She knows that there is new life stirring within her womb. She brings forth an egg, her most subjective truth as a woman. For a moment she holds it close to her, only to have it torn away by a muscular young man in football uniform. Identifying it as a football, and as his, at that, he darts down the field with it, dashing it heedlessly against a goal post . . . scoring his points, but annihilating the living contents of the woman's egg."

How quickly a woman's truth can be torn away from her! She may be unaware of how competitively she wages a discussion, how eager she is to score points as she dominates a conversation. And whenever a new sense of life emerges within her, it is stolen and broadcast to the throng, rather than being held within and pondered in her heart.

A woman speaks earnestly of her work and growth:

"I was grateful to hear the recording of the meeting with the new faculty . . . to hear, in my own voice, all that I have disliked in authorities from my past . . . everything in bold brush strokes, rather than with the nuance and sensitivity that I know I am capable of. It was not my Feminine ego leading the meeting at all, but my animus in a skirt.

"The faces around the table came back to me. I could see the pain in both the men and the women caused by that masculinized caricature of myself. I turned the recording machine off, suffering the usual recrimination from my inner judges. Then I remembered how little voice I had had in the past and forgave my bravado mode. Perhaps it had seemed better than having no voice at all!

"Rather than let my Masculine side criticize me from within, I asked for a new voice of constancy and prevailing, the modes I wished to affirm in the teachers under my direction. I wanted to speak as a woman.

"I knew that I needed to relate from my grounded Feminine ego. I worked with my convictions, solidifying here, softening there. Suddenly I was filled with the feelings that had been pushed away, with how much I cared for the work, for the children that we teachers all loved.

"At the next meeting I put the agenda aside and simply spoke from my heart."

A second woman speaks:

"Old friends never understood the difficulty I had coming into my own. Great-grandmother was still stylish and slender at ninety and a brilliant conversationalist. She corrected us all on grammar and accuracy of detail. All of the family women were expected to be like her . . . only our brightness was acknowledged!

"Although I had gone far professionally, I was often disappointed in my public presentations. I knew that my crisp, amusing style rarely touched the women in the audience.

"One evening, as I spoke, an image came to me of a spectator at a tennis match, focusing on me for only an instant, then on the opposite court, as I began a sentence

from within myself and listened, helpless, while my other voice completed it in an opposite mode. I could speak for only a moment before my Masculine side stole the spotlight, engaging with the women in the audience so convincingly that I ended up addressing only their Masculine side.

"That night I dreamed of Great-grandmother, victorious in a tennis outfit. I knew that I must find a mentor from the Feminine realm.

"I went to the most deeply developed woman I knew, feeling confused and ashamed. She did not try to bring me to clarity, but asked me to wait within the confusion until a clarity emerged, rather than imposing it from the outside. 'Perhaps,' she said quietly, 'your great-grandmother's style was perfect to express her own life . . . but is not adequate to express yours.'

"The woman gave a permission I had not been granted before. In the next series of presentations, I let myself speak from my muddle. Groping and ponderous as it was, I knew that I was being deeply received, for the first time, by the women listeners."

A third woman, sits in reflection before she begins to speak:

"My own experience has been so different, perhaps because I am older. I had begun to write of our individuation process as women. Acquaintances asked how the work was progressing and asked if they might see it.

"After only a few pages were read, the protests quickly began: Very nice work, indeed, but it must be reframed. The line is too fine, too lunar. It must be bolder, more declarative. It needs a completely different voice!

"Footsteps retreated down the driveway . . . car doors slammed shut.

"That weekend I lay in bed with flu, feverish and lost. The outer situation mirrored the chaos within . . . a female cardinal flew against the window, hour after hour, with a dull thud.

"My heart hurt under my ribs, and if I had not known so well how my body has always expressed my emotional pain, I would have feared that I was suffering a heart attack. With the fever, scenes of failure from my whole life passed before my eyes. 'Weighed in the balances and found wanting,' thundered my old inner judges . . . 'the wrong mode . . . the wrong way . . . wrong.' As wrong-headed as that lady cardinal hurtling herself against the window.

"As I neared the very bottom of the chaos, I heard only the last sentence from several days before: 'It needs a different voice . . . a completely different voice.'

"My heart grew quieter. With the grey dawn came a solitary whisper . . . 'But this is my voice!' I had laboured so long to develop its steadfast measure and balance, worked so diligently to quietly bring it forth. This was the only voice I had. There was no other.

"I slept.

"In the days that followed, I chastised myself many times. Why was I not more forthright, bolder, as the acquaintances asked? Why was I . . . only as I was? And then a memory came of a painful, patriarchal attitude. It was an attitude that invalidated a woman as she sought to express her subtle awareness as woman . . . left her struggling to bring forth her subjective experience in a hull of objectivity, an empty shell of words.

" 'No wonder,' I thought, 'that a woman sometimes adopts a Masculine voice as she speaks. No wonder she loses touch with her most poignant feeling values. And, worst of all, no wonder that a woman so often speaks her truth in a voice that is not her own . . . leaves her deepest Feminine wisdom mute, unvoiced, unheard.'

"The flu lingered several days. At last I felt well enough to be back in the woods one afternoon towards dusk. The light was soft . . . the late-winter woods, subtle hues of browns and greys.

"I sat for a long time watching the branches silhouetted against the darkening sky. Slowly, a tired awareness emerged within me . . . that all I wanted to do in my lifetime was to try to speak my truth as woman . . . to say it in my own voice."

I sit listening to the wind.
   . . . the wind listens back to me.

How might your life have been different if, as a young woman struggling to find your voice ... in despair that you might never be able to say what you knew inside ... there had been a place for you to begin to speak as a woman?

If you had been received into a circle of women, and during the silence, the women had let you speak ... had let you speak over and over, as your words slowly came together? If they had listened deeply and attentively to your emerging voice ... had noted your tenacity and tenderness ... your steadfastness and resolve.

And you had seen, in the faces of the women seated there in the circle ... in the still older faces of the women standing slightly behind them in the shadows ... the pride and respect the older women felt as they heard the truth in your young woman's voice.

How might your life be different?

A sense of sacredness

The wind softens . . .
    . . . winter thaws.

In earliest springtime of each year, a group of women gathered in a small mountain town where there was a healing spring. It had become their custom to repair to the baths for purification and cleansing. They offered up any malady or woundedness to the powerful mineral waters.

For several years, whenever the group gathered, a ritual had taken place. As the women first assembled, a candle was lighted and a small statue placed in its light. It was a figure of a woman, wrought in brass and bronze, her hair a twisted braid of burnished copper down her back.

The statue had been found at the bottom of a chest brought back from India by the missionary great-uncle of one of the women. In the circle cast by the candle, the presence of the statue drew the women back in time . . . to a time, long ago, when the earth was still held sacred . . . to a way of being with the earth and their own Feminine nature that the women had not lived out, but dimly sensed within themselves, waiting to be reborn.

The women gathered throughout the year in several different places. There was a concern that the statue would be damaged in travel. A small, silken bag was sewn to protect it, and another, of a sturdier fabric, as covering for the first. Eventually, a third was added. The statue was well protected.

At the opening of each retreat, the yarn holding the bags was slowly untied and the statue carefully placed at the center of the circle. Every springtime, the woman who led the group gave each woman a gift to help keep the power of the ritual alive within her throughout the coming year.

The small cloth bags given that springtime as remembrances of the ritual were replicas of the bags holding the statue. The gifts were placed on the pillows at night while the women slept. The first woman to awaken and open her gift came in quietly to say her thanks for her "first and only Goddess bag." She wondered aloud how she would fill it. The name seemed fitting, and the gifts were remembered as "the Goddess bags."

Later that same morning, the women sat on a terrace looking out over the woods. They spoke of the meaning, for each of them, of receiving the empty bag. What would each woman place into it from her own uniqueness and life?

A woman prepared to speak, brushed a strand of dark hair from her face:

"I offer into this bag the whole of my life as woman ...joy and suffering both ... all that is sacred to me: the smooth, flat stone from the day on the beach when my husband last told me he loved me, a few days before he died ... The old damask napkin from the day I took tea with my great-grandmother, when she was ninety-two ... Two dried flowers, the red, from the day my first daughter was born, and the lavender, from the day I thought I would die from the pain of her death."

The woman bowed her head. The women sat in silence around her, as witness to her pain.

The youngest woman spoke, her chestnut hair aglow in the soft spring light:

"Suddenly, I see the depth of the woundedness in my womanhood. I would not have thought, before, of honouring our sorrows or valuing our wounds . . . of holding anything of the Feminine sacred. I realize that those of us so wounded will suffer the gravest doubts in placing anything of ourselves into the silken bag.

"I offer up the wounding in my Masculine side. My fears, when I was young, that I could not achieve in the world. And, later, an opposite wound, as my life was devoured by work. I offer up the one-sided judgement that keeps me, even now, from respecting my own suffering, that fills me, instead, with shame for ever having suffered . . . shame, failure, and condemnation for having done my whole life wrong."

A slender woman listened, hand on her grey-blonde hair:

"I pray that we offer up our habitual denigration of our own Feminine nature . . . the denigration of ourselves that leaves us unable or unwilling to endure suffering, even the suffering necessary to discover our own souls.

"I offer up the impatience that makes us try to rip forth full-blown the answers to our lives, rather than trusting them to bring themselves forth from the Self in their own time. I offer this up and pray that a sense of quiet forbearance may be returned to us all."

The sun was low in the sky. The wind blew softly through the nearby trees.

The oldest woman began to speak, fell silent . . . sighed:

"I didn't expect to live so long, to see such change before I died. I place into this bag a wounding that I see in woman after woman, a wounding of great poignancy to me: a pushing and pressing at ourselves, a coldness towards our own pain . . . an expectation of ourselves to be invulnerable. I feel a deep concern for the lack of human kindness that I see among us . . . for an attitude that meets suffering from a safe, crisp platform of solutions rather than witnessing its truth from within our own experience of pain."

The slanting rays of the setting sun shone on her silver hair. *"I offer into this silken bag all that has been most scorned of the Archetypal Feminine realm. May it be redeemed and healed and become the most sacred contents of the bag."*

I sit listening to the wind . . . and wonder how the silken bag will be filled. What will each woman offer into it that reflects an image to herself as daughter to the Great Mother?

I sit listening . . . and wonder if the bag of the Goddess, also, is being filled anew . . . filled with a new sense of the Feminine that can heal and sustain us all.

I listen . . . and wonder if the bag of all of us awaits, again, to be filled?

I sit in wonder
  . . . spring returns.

How might your life have been different if, once, as you sat in silence in your place of reflection, someone had given you a small silken bag...and invited you to fill it from your conscious woundedness...from your deepest awareness as woman...and lastly, from your joy?

If, as you raised your eyes, you had seen the Great Goddess on a hillside
   ...gleaning
      ...gleaning with her daughters
         ...gleaning through the measureless epochs of time

   ...for a renewed sense
         of the sacred Feminine,
               and you knew that you would join them
                  to fill the bag anew.

How might your life be different?

Woman
  sitting on a hillside
    listening . . .
      listening
        as the wind
          . . . blows its eternal questions:

        How can woman
          help her daughters
            find their ancient ground?

And the earth
   sings her response:

          Find it yourself...
                 ...yourself.

HER WORK
WITH THE MASCULINE
WITHIN HER

Welcoming her energy

I sit listening for the wind
. . . a May breeze murmurs from the meadow
. . . wafts of lilies-of-the-valley
. . . memories of spring commencements.

A circle of women of many ages gathered in the bright spring sunlight, young women in cap and gown, their mothers and their teachers. A slender, blonde woman stood up, adjusted her doctoral robe. She briefly touched the hands of the women seated next to her and looked at the young women around her:

"We mothers and teachers have gathered this circle, hoping to share our experience in the animus realm with you younger women. What an exciting time for you! You have marshalled this wonderful energy to complete your studies, prepare for your professions."

She nodded towards the black woman sitting nearest her, also in doctoral robes:

"We were remembering how it felt as our Masculine energy first appeared: our lofty over-spiritualized longings . . . our beautiful adolescent hero-worship of brilliant and beloved teachers . . . our sense of justice emerging . . . and our fearsome goal-directedness!"

As a young girl begins to grow up, a new energy emerges within her. It brings bursting energies, powers of concentration not present to her before. She experiences a clarity and purposefulness, an ability to discipline her efforts that give her a sense of power as she seeks to distinguish herself in academics, athletics, artistry . . . in all areas of achievement and accomplishment.

At this time, the daughter needs to separate from the mother to develop her inner Masculine powers. She must cut her roots from the Feminine ground and make a fearful crossing to the Masculine. During this crossing, the animus draws the girl farther away from the Feminine than she will ever be.

Encouragement from the Masculine realm is necessary, at this time, for the girl, for this energy is her newly developing inner Masculine side. The support of father or another appropriate male is essential, especially if the mother has not had opportunity to work with her own inner Masculine energy. For the girl needs a Masculine role model in the outer world. Its absence might be reflected in exaggerated awe of the Masculine or in an abstractedness that does not allow the girl to ground herself, in a vacuum rather than a solidity in her feelings for herself as a woman.

"When women professionals of our age were growing up," the blonde woman continued, *"we identified with our fathers or male teachers. I didn't want anything to do with the diffuse Feminine consciousness of my mother or her friends."*

The black woman by her side interrupted laughingly:

"I'm sure that I was headstrongly anti-feminine as I identified with my Masculine side. I was enjoying its power, and I was strutting its stuff!"

35

Then she smiled across the circle at her own daughter in cap and gown:

"How fortunate you are now as young women who have the support and understanding of mothers who consciously went through these stages of development themselves.

"If the mother can remember that her daughter's struggle is against the entire Feminine realm, and not against her personally, she may be able to provide a container for the struggle that is broad enough that her daughter will not need to make a complete schism between them.

"By lending loving support, the mother may even be allowed to act as mentor for the emerging energy in her daughter . . . may provide compass, charts, and sea anchor for her daughter's maiden voyage through these troubled and murky waters . . . be allowed, perhaps, to guide what may finally emerge as radiant qualities of leadership and excellence in her daughter's adult womanhood.

"If the mother is unclear in her own relationship with her Masculine side, unable to develop her talents or to find her voice, the situation may be terribly painful for all. The Masculine energy will set itself out in chaotic disruption of the relationship, as mother and daughter are locked into a power struggle, turning household peace into a shambles. Mother will be unable to understand or tolerate the undirected energy in her daughter . . . will dig in her heels on the old issues of a clean room and a modest demeanour. And the girl will be scathing in her criticism of the mother."

Another woman interrupted, visibly upset:

"If only there had been someone to help my mother and me! We were terrible to each other. I needed her love, and I

think she needed mine. How I wish there had been someone to give us some understanding of what was going on!"

The black woman nodded sympathetically:

"It would have helped your mother if she had understood that it was temporarily your task to overthrow all of her values, as you explored the exciting new energy emerging within yourself.

"A mother must know, in her heart, that she represents the very ground of womanhood to which her daughter will later return, this time no longer grafted onto and sustained by the roots of the mother, but striking root, herself, in the ancient Feminine ground.

"The mother may be the only one with patience and steadiness enough to help the girl with her obstreperous young animus. If the father tries to deal with this unruly side of the daughter, he may lock into combat with the young Masculine aspect of the girl, competing and needing to conquer it. Or, his own inner Feminine side, if he has ignored or neglected it, may engage in a petulant protest against the daughter's Masculine side. Neither way is very hopeful for the girl's development."

The woman paused in thought . . . then slowly reached out to touch the lilac by her side:

"I marvel when I remember how wonderfully my mother handled this stage of my growing up. She fostered the relationship between my father and me, made the natural attraction between us feel safe, and helped him provide a good role model for the Masculine side of me. She encouraged Father to listen to me, to help me draw my thoughts together, even to take a stance.

"Mother must have known how a girl's whole sense of herself can be affected by criticism, especially if it is stinging or harsh, how the animus will pick it up and undermine her with it for years to come. For she listened so caringly to my pain."

Two women from the circle stood to respond. The first spoke:

"My father and brothers saw me as competition . . . easy to beat down . . . a poor second to Father, fair game to all those brothers. And my mother saw me as a threat and threw up her hands. She abandoned me to the men . . . literally kicked me out of her kitchen and sewing room. I had no one to support me . . . no one . . . no encouragement from any direction.

"I became as tough as my brothers . . . merciless to myself. And my critical inner voice is still as nasty to me as they were. To this day, I can feel the pain of that period of my life. It comes out in rebelliousness and rage, in feeling that I can't do anything anyhow, so why try? I am learning, only now, to marshall my energies and abilities in a way that gives meaning to my life. And I'm scared for the time my three little girls will need me to befriend, in them, what was never befriended in me."

The second woman spoke:

"I was wonderfully fortunate to have had the opposite experience. A professor acknowledged me in class as I sat amidst my peers. I had presented a short paper on Aeschylus. As I finished reading, the professor looked straight at me and said, 'Miss ____, you have a keen and subtle mind.' He was a wonderful model for the Masculine side of myself. That happened nearly forty years ago and still is the basis for my sense of my own skills."

A white-haired woman had joined the circle midway through the morning. She had lingered at the Grandmothers' Tea earlier, across the meadow.

"In my girlhood, if a woman married young, it was expected that her energies and abilities would be fulfilled by her husband. Only if it was clear that he could not fulfill them was she allowed to fulfill them herself.

"There were stories, told humourously but with a tragic overtone, of women, reluctant to take up their own development, who projected it onto their sons—'my son, the doctor'—burdening the boy with what his mother might have fulfilled.

"But today, something else often occurs, as the mother's undeveloped Masculine side identifies with that side of her daughter and the mother attaches to the girl's goal- and achievement-drive. The mother may spur the daughter on in single-minded effort towards success in the outer realm while she rejects the daughter's needs in the inner realm of the Feminine.

"Then, the old story of the mother living through her son becomes even more tragic as the mother lives through the Masculine side of her daughter and prevents the girl from striking root in the Feminine ground."

The breeze softly freshened . . . wafted an almost unbearable fragrance of lily-of-the-valley. The women stirred in their circle . . . fell silent to listen again.

The slender, blonde woman who had begun the morning drew it to a close:

"We offer our love and congratulations to you young women and hope that what we have learned can help you on your way."

Then she paused, tears sparkling in her eyes:

"And when the time comes for each of you to lovingly help your daughter begin her inner work, let her know that we respect her struggle . . . that we have struggled, too. And that we welcome her with a deep sense of belonging . . . to herself . . . to you, her mother . . . and to the entire Feminine realm."

How might your life have been different if, once when you were a young girl . . . worried about your studies and still wanting to be helpful at home . . . your mother had quietly looked at you, one evening, and said, "It's all right, dear, I'll clear the table tonight. I know that you have a test tomorrow. Go, do what you need to prepare . . . and take a little time for yourself."

And if she had said, very softly, with a smile,
" . . . later, let's look at the moon together
    . . . there's a lovely spring breeze blowing."

How might your life be different?

Embracing her encounter

The wind blows
 . . . blows insistently.
  Windmills spin.
   A live tree topples over.

I sit listening . . . and I wonder how to share my concern as I see the dilemma of so many of us women today. We have harnessed the Masculine energy within ourselves so well. Yet, we do not seem to know how to "turn the wind off."

Until a woman becomes aware of the Masculine energy within and consciously engages with it, it remains an autonomous force, out of her control. It keeps her focused on all that is outside of herself, rather than on being and becoming who she truly is. The complete absence of Masculine energy would leave a deathly stillness, no breath to breathe in her life. But how does she learn to engage with and to consciously work with this energy, rather than to simply be blown about by it?

A few years ago, a group of women gathered to talk about working with their Masculine side. I did not know if talking about it as an intellectual idea would work. The discussion progressed from the women's personal experiences to ever more airy abstractions. By the end of the afternoon, we disbanded in disarray. For we had been taken over by the very side of ourselves that we had been trying to discuss. How were we going to learn to work with this perplexing side of ourselves?

The women agreed to try again, but this time to share only their subjective and personal experiences. The first to speak was a woman of robust and hearty demeanour:

"I was raised quite traditionally. My mother knew nothing of her inner Masculine energy. On good days, everything seemed rosy for us, nice little women staying in our places. We identified completely with patriarchal views, did all the expected things, expressed the accepted attitudes. We were docile, prosily complacent, and satisfied with ourselves... frighteningly unaware of our own existence as women.

"But on bad days, in a black mood, I stood at the kitchen sink, dishcloth idly in hand... or stared listlessly over the copy machine, out of my office window. The Masculine energy appeared in my dreams as an intruder breaking in at the door. That energy burst impulsively into my daily life... banging at pots and pans, tearing at the garden, pounding at my typewriter, or scolding at my husband.

"I know now that a woman's relationship with the Masculine within deeply colours her relationships with the men around her. But I didn't know that, then, and I saw the same qualities of roguish aloofness in every man I met, without realizing that those were the qualities of the Masculine side of myself. I felt the same kind of criticism and rejection from men who were really judgemental as well as from my own loving sons. That negative Masculine energy even came back at me as criticism from the harsher side of my women friends."

The woman put her hands to her face: *"I wonder if there is a single one of us who has not felt attacked by the untamed animus in a woman friend?... or who has not seen the destructive power of that side of herself as it attacks her husband or her own womanly feelings?"*

The woman nearest her silently put her hand on the woman's shoulder. *"I began to realize that it was my task to harness that energy within myself . . . or it would blow undirected and devastate all in its path.*

"So I tried to engage consciously with that side of myself. But my animus called out heavy artillery: I was assailed by criticism from within and without."

A second woman interrupted excitedly. She held up a yellowed newspaper clipping pasted in her journal.

"I cut this out many years ago and labelled it 'The Energy of the Animus United Against the Woman, as She Begins Her Work.' It is a frightening picture. Nine or ten men in a close cadre . . . faces twisted into snarls, full of accusation . . . they glared at the eye of the camera, and out of the paper at me.

"That picture reflected perfectly the Masculine energy within me, full of insults and judgment, as I began my inner encounter. All the men in the photograph seemed to glower at the camera, for the Masculine side of me did not want to be exposed, but wanted to control me and not have its power threatened."

A very young woman listened thoughtfully, then began to speak:

"I began my encounter, not with my own inner Masculine side, but with that part in my dearest woman friend. She had been pushing herself too hard and was hurtful and impatient with me. I asked her to sit down for a moment while I told her how miserable that side of her was making all of us, driving away her boyfriend and even me. I told her how much we loved her and asked if, somehow, we could help her return to herself.

44

"This probably was not the recommended way to begin, but it seemed to help. I spoke as gently and caringly as I could, and she was able to cry. Later, she told me I had helped her to see her harsher side more clearly."

An older woman reached out to touch the younger woman's hand:

"Recommended or not, we begin however we can. I, also, began the encounter with the Masculine side of myself without really knowing how. I was having difficulty settling into a sense of my life, was constantly distracted by goals in opposite directions, expectations of perfection from myself. I felt as if something was at me from within, and I had to communicate with it.

"So, in a fantasy, I summoned all of the Masculine figures from my dreams to come to a council. Later, realizing that there might be a nicer way, I invited them formally and politely, as ambassadors and couriers, and even set out colourful banners and flags to mark their seats.

"I asked the threatening figures, those appearing as marauders and bandits, to be willing to change. Then I earnestly requested the most encouraging figures, old teachers or mentors from my past, to take the others in hand, as a knight prepares a squire, teaching him to serve with devotion and honour.

"I told them it was my life as a woman that was to be lived, and that their cooperation and energy were needed. I charged them all with a trust to be my knight-protectors and aides, then embraced each one, in spirit, and offered my warmest thanks.

"The encounter brought a change in my relationship with my Masculine energy. I have a feeling that the dialogue will go on all my life. Yet, I have begun to be hopeful as the

Masculine figures in my dreams begin to show a recognition of my womanhood and my needs. And in daily life, I am clearer with myself and in my relationships with men."

The wind blows . . . the years slip past.

Slowly over the years, a woman's awareness of herself deepens as, again and again, she re-enters her encounter with the Masculine energy within. If she can be clear in her Feminine values, yet respectful of her Masculine side, it will make the decisive turn towards her to serve as her faithful knight.

Most importantly, a woman needs to know that it is only her deepest feelings that will finally convince this energy to separate from society's values and to serve her own life.

A woman dreamed:

I am being judged by a group of men.

Knowing that I can dance it out to help them understand, I go to the end of the room.

I dance, passionately dance, drumming my convictions on the floor. Deep within me I know that all I can depend upon, as convincement for those men, is the strength, power, and truth of my feelings as a woman.

How might it have been different for you, when you were at odds with your closest friends ... confused and in conflict within, if there had been a place for you, where you could be received by a woman whom you respected? And she listened as you told her how cut off you felt from yourself.

If the woman had quietly laid a fire and slowly begun to teach you a strange, new kind of dialogue ... writing your thoughts and feelings to the cut-off part of yourself that did not seem to understand ... then to sit in silence, listening for a response. And you had been surprised at how that mysterious other part of you listened ... and amazed to hear its answer!

And, as the fire burned low, you sat hugging your journal ... knowing you had just begun an encounter that would continue all of your life.

How might your life be different?

Bringing forth her feeling values

The wind blows so insistently
I cannot hear the earth
erupting underneath.
Cut off, I listen
. . . listen.

When a woman uses her energy only to reinforce what is outside of herself, she becomes cut off from her depths. Her own feelings and values become inaccessible to her. She molds herself to external values and loses touch with her individuality. She is cut off from all that is uniquely hers, from all that could nourish her and those around her, cut off from the creative, new answers within her so badly needed in the world today. Cut off from her deeper sense of life, from the wisdom of her own unconscious, she lives in an arid, approvable way.

And her depths become enraged!

The whole wellspring of womanly creativity within her is furious for not being tapped. And the greater the individuality and insight that have been dammed up, the greater the rage. For what is within must flow out: her feelings and life values, all that she cares about and knows, most deeply, to be true.

Four women sat in a rough cabin sheltered from the turbulent wind. They spoke of the difficulty of women in knowing or expressing themselves. The first woman had returned from a journey:

"I was aware of the anguish of women in areas where I travelled . . . women unable to express their feelings or bring forth their Feminine values. I thought of an old text, hidden away for centuries before it re-emerged . . . of being saved by bringing forth all that is within ourselves . . . or of being destroyed by forbidding what is within to come forth.

"I remembered a more ancient bringing forth as woman during the mensis, closest then to her own nature, knelt on the earth to offer it the gift of her own blood. She offered herself to the cycles of nature . . . knowing that nature would respond and pour forth its blessings in return.

"I wondered if we women might offer our blood again, in a figurative way . . . trusting that life itself will pour forth its gifts in response. That it will replenish our society with the Feminine values that are so cut off . . . values of devotion to the earth and to the individual . . . the values of the deeper Self."

An older woman paused in thought before she began to speak:

"My surroundings were very traditional, yet I managed to get an education, in spite of the attitudes against it. I found work within the given structure . . . it was my 'Cleft in the Rock.' At least it offered survival, though little personal space.

"But I knew I had ignored my feelings when I dreamed of a woman, so full of frustration and fatigue, that she could only lean her forehead against the door frame . . . hold it there, mute and tearless . . . unable to enter or leave. And later, of a woman's body crushed amidst rocks . . . the rocks of a bloodless, impersonal system that could never make room for me . . . never make room for anything from the Feminine realm."

The third woman, thirty years younger, a painter and musician, recalled her own ancestry:

"They were a black-garbed religious group that required strict conformity of behaviour and belief. I had been so taught to disregard my feelings that I never knew what I felt . . . playing every phrase to someone else's cadence.

"One day as I painted, all the passion of my blocked womanhood poured out onto the canvas in bold reds and oranges. I took out my cello and played to the painting. Then my whole body joined in a primitive dance.

"Again and again, with arms flung wide, I danced my feelings out, until every cell of my being knew that I was alive . . . alive to the joy and intensity within me . . . alive to myself, to life."

Suddenly the women rushed to the window. An old wall lay toppled before the changing wind. When they returned to their seats, the fourth woman began to speak:

"My grandmother, my mother, and me . . . only allowed to smile and agree . . . only able to affirm what was initiated around us . . . never able to initiate ourselves.

"If my grandmother ever felt so strongly that she protested a situation, she became hysterical. And my mother ricocheted between the hysterical and an opinionated voice, with no grounded Feminine ego between them . . . enraged that the men could never hear what she was unable to say.

"I was caught in those modes, completely cut off from myself. Depressed, with no energy for the causes I had served only half a year before! And my inner Masculine side did its foul double-play, damning me for my depression, then berating me for having served so long what had not served me. All those generations of women in my lineage using our energies

in service to a system that had so little awareness of separate Feminine values!"

The woman spoke with a quiet intensity, gripping the arms of her chair: *"A woman counsellor came. She asked me to trust my feelings, even my depression, as my deepest truth. She asked me to respect my rage, not identify with it . . . to honour it as holding within itself all of the ancient Feminine, so long dormant, neglected . . . forbidden, for so long, to come forth.*

"She asked me to stay with my pain, not let my animus invalidate it . . . helped me shriek it in wordless, guttural cries . . . paeans of despair to the gods:
> *the anguish of suppressed feeling values*
> > *of my mother and her mother before her,*
> > > *of lost devotion to matter,*
> > > > *lost Feminine sovereignty,*
> > > > > *of rain-forests felled,*
> > > > > > *waters spilt with oil,*
> > > > > > > *. . . the anguish of the earth herself.*

"She asked me to imagine the significance if woman could heal the split between her inner Masculine development and her unlistened-to womanly values . . . the significance if each woman would be willing to consciously suffer her own share of the anguish that says something is vastly wrong in the values of this world today.

"She asked me to imagine the significance if each woman were willing to bear the pain and isolation that must be endured, each time, to bring our values to expression . . . to imagine the significance if each woman would pour out her devotion as our ancient sisters poured out their blood . . . pour out our passion and devotion and await the response . . . as the ancient Feminine Archetype brings forth her values anew."

51

A woman's dream:

Near the edge of a woods a group gathers, hushed and reverent. Suddenly there is a tremor . . . a pulsating beneath the surface. From cracks and crevices, blood erupts from the earth . . . rises aloft to the heavens . . . returns to the earth as rain.

The group throngs into the clearing. With heads upturned and arms outstretched, they raise a solemn cry . . . "The blood has returned to the land!"

How might your life be different, if there were a place for you to go, whenever you feel overwhelmed by the power of your feelings? If you could be received by women gathered in a circle and helped to witness your feelings ... and to trust their truth?

If the women would build up the fire and let you dance out your feelings ... your pain and anguish and hurt ... even your wordless rage?

And, as the fire burned low and you rested from your dance, you could look into the glowing embers ... and wonder how it might have been different for your mother and grandmother before you, if they had been received by women, long before you were born. If women then could have helped them to trust that their feelings served a purpose ... could have helped them believe that they might bring truth to bear where it was needed?

How might the lives of all of us be different?

Honouring her intuition

The wind blows clouds across
the strange, dark face of the moon
. . . hardly there at all
against the last, piercing rays of the sun.

The element of the Feminine most difficult to comprehend is the lunar spirituality of our Feminine intuition . . . the strange, ineffable beauty of the dark face of the moon. The intuition, by nature ephemeral, is easily dismissed. What our intuition grasps cannot be held in the hand. Moreover, modern society places little value on "things unseen." Yet somehow woman's intuition must communicate her Feminine vision to a society that could perish without it.

If older women around her are not grounded in values of the Feminine, they will be unable to help the younger woman bring forth her intuitive gift. Her Masculine energy will undermine any intuitive experience she has, point out the superior achievement of others in more identifiable realms. She will feel that her gifts are nebulous and insubstantial, tell herself she should have been a financier, or at least a gourmet cook.

The intuitive woman is caught between two aspects of the animus. On the one side, the Judging Patriarch invalidates her subjective experience. He holds up before her already-established ethical and spiritual systems, makes no room for her uniquely personal intuitive gift. The more vibrantly the woman's vision presses to emerge, the more vehemently the Patriarch thunders: "WE WILL CONDEMN YOU IF YOU DARE TO SPEAK YOUR TRUTH!"

The woman may object, but not be able to say in words what she senses intuitively is not right. She will continually join groups that do not recognize her intuition and be cast in the role of the rebel . . . while the fresh new voice and direction of her vision, so crucially needed by the group, will be unable to emerge.

On the other side of the intuitive woman is the worst sort of Peter Pan, who forever refuses to grow up. If her intuition speaks directly of the Feminine spirit, the Peter Pan within her engages in a frenzy of activity to keep her from bringing it forth. Rather than helping her to develop her gifts so that she can challenge the established order, he interrupts her self-discipline with distractions in every direction.

The inner Peter Pan makes the woman see her own abilities in others rather than in herself. Dapper and debonair, he runs her all over town to lectures and workshops, seeking outside herself the depths she cannot own within . . . keeps her an admiring disciple of the vision she sees in others. Finally, he drops her at her doorstep, empty and exhausted.

There is no other choice for the intuitive woman but to connect with the Self within, for the spiritual aspect of the intuitive is the most important part of her nature. If either her Judging Patriarch or her immature Peter Pan prevents the woman from forming a relationship with the deeper Self, she is left hollow, robbed of her essence. She will feel invalidated and will appear airy and drifty . . . be unable to bring her vision to clarity or expression.

And here lies the terrible struggle: the more distinctly Feminine a woman's intuition, the more it lingers in shadow beside the brightness of her inner Masculine side. The subtler her gift, the greater her struggle to bring it forth: the animus will make it seem hardly there at all.

One woman's drawing showed this struggle: a delicate dark line on an otherwise empty page . . . a woman's face in profile, one tear falling on her cheek. She named her drawing *"The Nothing Against the Something,"* the ephemeral lunar quality of woman's intuitive nature . . . elusive, mute, and weeping . . . impossible to articulate.

In spite of the terrible struggle, woman must realize how deeply her intuitive gift is needed in our world today! When a society is not nourished by a sense of the deeper Self inside each individual, it can easily be taken over. Oppressive mass belief systems appear that lead to barrenness and spiritual sterility.

The intuition of woman is needed to provide a connection to the transcendent Self . . . a connection that is subjective and unique to each individual. A woman must take courage to work with her vision, however fragmentary. She must take her animus by the hand, ask its aid to mediate the unseen, and request its help to express the freshness of her vision to her society.

Three women spoke of their lives and work. The first woman spoke of her father, a powerful political figure whose criticism, even in her adult womanhood, was more difficult for her because of his prominence in the world:

"There was no one to help me understand all that was inside me. The only realities recognized by my family were the polls and the press. All of Mother's energy went to Father's support.

"As a child, I thought I was crazy as I saw behind the scenes and listened underneath. And, as an adult, I was terrified that what I knew intuitively could never come to expression, but would perish . . . a strangled scream.

"Only in the hospital, recovering from a breakdown, did a quiet nurse confirm for me the power of healing touch flowing in my hands. She taught me how to breathe to nourish that energy. I have learned, these past few years, to work with my healing touch ... to hold it as my little shred of truth against my inner critical voice. My family may very well always view me as bizarre, but my hands and intuition finally know what they know. And my children and garden are flourishing."

The second woman, only daughter in a large family, was from a religious group in which her father was leader:

"My father was extremely articulate, but I could never express myself. It was as if I spoke a non-existent language ... and had to translate my formlessness into words I did not know.

"If I voiced my curiosity about why things were as they were, my mother became upset. The attitude of the religious group was that anything not already codified must not really exist. They had no realization that their prevailing consciousness simply could not comprehend the emergent mysteries of the Archetypal Feminine realm.

"I could never understand why my brother's gifts were recognized, while my intuitive gift was not valued by the hierarchy ... even though similar intuitive abilities were acknowledged in the founders of our group.

"I became alienated and identified with the only things left to me — my individuality and intuition. Just as I was about to identify completely with my gifts, in a grandiose negative way, I was sent far away to study.

"It was a mixed blessing . . . I felt terribly outcast, but I came under the influence of several deeply developed women who had met a similar adverse situation in their own lives or the lives of their daughters. Their warmth and intelligence grounded me. They somehow saw my gifts . . . helped me bring them forth with wondrous silken materials . . . through colour and design.

"I returned home, accepting my intuitive gift as both grace and burden. But my struggle was not yet over. I married a man as negating as my own father had been. My husband denied the truth of my intuition, blocking any chance of my expressing it. My body reflected the situation exactly: a huge tumor, not malignant, yet totally blocking the flow of life in the Feminine parts.

"My Masculine side, in its usual pattern, created conflict with my current group. Too depleted to struggle, I released the outer world and turned to my creative inner world, so alive with swirling dyes and iridescent silks.

"Releasing the negating exterior allowed transformation to begin. Helpful teachers appeared who affirmed my gifts: women who had suffered the same ostracism I had, and a man who provided a positive role model for my Masculine side. As their kindness softened my pain, I could accept the stigma of not having fulfilled the dogmas of the religious group of my birth . . . could admit that I had never been a docile little girl in a setting where that was the only path allowed for the female children.

"At last, I realized that I had to give up hoping for outer acceptance. My new teachers helped me see that, early in my life, the strong voice of the Self within had somehow created my difficulty, had caused the same unsettling vividness of colour in my girlhood questions as in my luminous silks.

"I stopped trying to translate the voice within me into the language of everyday, but finally learned to speak from the chaos and truth of the vision within me and trust that I would be heard!"

The third woman was an artist and poet. Her work touched people deeply. Yet she struggled with an animus that dismissed her gifts with patronizing half-interest:

"My Masculine side reflected so clearly the men in my family lineage. They were men of power in the world, men who found women charming and curious but of little consequence beyond that. There was no comprehension of a deeper Feminine nature . . . no tolerance for darkness, no acceptance of suffering in any form whatever.

"My mother never felt she was taken seriously. She suffered greatly whenever my father, an admiral, was called to sea. She fought cancer valiantly throughout my girlhood.

"Mother's illness left a terrible void. For in her efforts to fulfill family patterns that denied illness and darkness, she simply vanished whenever her suffering become acute . . . without a word to her children. Shortly before her death, she disappeared for the last time, leaving me with a black hole of terror that I would disappear, too.

"Although I graduated from Harvard, my overly rational Masculine side still did not let me value my gift. I was left empty and ungrounded, for my intuitive truth was the core of my Feminine nature . . . my animus would not grant recognition to my most essential part!

"I tried to fill the hollow by studying philosophy and religion, the vision and truth of others. But even then, my animus intervened in an insidious way, convincing me that my family needed me. I nicknamed myself 'Mrs. Always

Available' and imagined a Mother Rabbit, forever there on the porch, waving her apron amiably to welcome in husband and children . . . rarely able to bid adieu to have quiet time for herself.

"Two decades later, I fought cancer myself, just as Mother had . . . and desperate attacks of panic and terror that I would disappear before I could express what was locked inside.

"In an effort to confront my illness, I began to paint the anguish caused as my Masculine side rejected my deepest Feminine nature. A man's face appeared on the canvas ascending in a flame, haughty and aloof. For months I railed prayerfully against this inner negation.

"Finally, a blessed sign of transformation came, the figure of a black Christ in a dream: the Masculine who knew of suffering, who knew the struggle to embrace one's own truth in the face of the establishment. At last the truth of my suffering was affirmed.

"Drawings and poetry poured forth! Other women reflected to me what they saw in my work. They recognized its darkly passionate, inchoate formlessness as their own inner experience, the intensity and chaos of woman's vision as it struggles against the light . . . the Nothing Against the Something so deep in the nature of the Feminine."

The wind blows,
the sky is in tumult.
Amidst the chaos and darkness,
. . . I listen.

How might your life have been different if, once long ago, when you were aware of stirrings within yourself, of something not yet emerged...there had been a place to go where you could sense the presence of an ancient Feminine wisdom? If you sat in the darkness watching as the fires were lighted...and saw the dancing shadows on the walls of the chamber...and were aware, again, of those stirrings within yourself that you could not express?

If the women gathered there around you had affirmed, with shining eyes, that your stirrings were a part of the Feminine most sacred and mysterious...that women of all epochs have instinctively known must remain forever free.

And if the women with you had told you that the courage of your vision and your struggle to express it would make a difference to women in ages after you...

How might your life be different?

Distinguishing her life

The wind drops,
the fragrance of fresh-mown hay
drifts across the fields
. . . the first harvest of late summer.

I sit listening . . . remembering a woman whose life was rich in harvest. Supervisor in a large state hospital, she was retiring, after many years of service, with recognition and honours. She received official citations . . . and a cat to keep her company.

Things seemed to be going smoothly. She redirected her energy from the hospital to her private practice . . . and tended the cat. Oh, perhaps she was working a bit more than she wished, she said, *"but things would even out."*

And, yet, the situation seemed to shift the other way.

Years before, she had known that her father, a man of the open plains, was terribly proud of his daughter . . . his sons came ten years later . . . and he worked to develop the skills and bravery of his golden-haired little girl. The story she remembered most poignantly, told with pride and pain, was of the day she had circled the house, at her father's command, to test her endurance and courage . . . barefoot in the snow.

As she grew, she went on to discipline herself in many different directions.

"I always did well in school. Like many women my age, I was taught to use the mind in a purely rational way, as if life could be figured out logically. But I had little under-standing or tolerance for my own needs for nurture or rest. My inner driving force allowed me as little softness as my father had. Once, during my marriage, I had my husband install light bulbs in the garden, so that I could weed far into the night.

"I have mourned so long the difficulty I have had in relating to women. As a young girl, my feeling needs were left confused and unsupported. I knew that mother was quite proud of my mind and accomplishments, but she related very little to the rest of my development. There was a deep well of undifferentiated feeling within me, full of pain and isolation, never recognized or affirmed by her.

"In my adolescence, I often felt perplexed as she set me the task of accomplishing her goals while she sat chatting cozily with my more girlish girlfriends. No wonder that, later, I was suspicious and fearful of betrayal by women. As much as I longed for closeness, I felt too alienated from the Feminine to allow myself to be deeply received.

"Even with my own children, there was sometimes difficulty. My daughter, especially, experienced me as an island of unrest, offering her nowhere to dock. Both my son and my daughter followed in my professional footsteps . . . I knew they respected my abilities. Yet, they spoke of feeling unreceived whenever they expressed concern for my personal well-being. After all, I had trained myself to manage with no regard from others . . . the girl who ran barefoot in the snow.

"The very efficiency and capability that had always served me so well, had, of course, been my undoing . . . my quiet time always stolen, since I was so able to cope. Stopped in

the hospital corridors by every troubled face, answering questions on the way to every single meeting, always arriving late! I was at war with time, plain old Chronos time . . . had no idea at all of what Kairos time was about.

"And then, one day, the cat ran away.

"Things came crashing down! I did not know how fond I had become of 'Mr. Cat' . . . realized only later that the formality of his name reflected an unwillingness to draw nearer to my own creature needs.

"Bereft, I began to bring my life back to myself. My body called loudly to me in the form of backaches and allergies.

"I knew that I had to free myself from the compulsive false energy of the animus that knows no natural tiredness. For the first time in my life, I became aware of my own needs for nurture and care. I began to give consideration to food, took time to prepare it thoughtfully. I arranged for a series of vigourous therapeutic massages . . . then, for a second series, gentler than the first.

"I made a promise to myself to accept no new patients . . . to give time, each day, to my journal. I dreamed of making the journey to hold my first grandchild in my arms . . . the daughter of my daughter.

"On the weekend, I walked by the river.

"I began to clear away the thousands of things I had saved, always waiting for the day I would take time to savour them. Dresses now too small . . . bought to give me a special feeling of myself as woman . . . that I never found occasion to wear. I folded them into a box and grieved for a side of myself never allowed to emerge.

"The books were the hardest to sort. I have always enjoyed reading, loved the world of ideas. But I realized there would never be time to discover my own ideas of life if I were to read all of those carefully saved words.

"I sorted a lifetime of papers.

"And now I am sorting out the way I learned to use my mind, a way devoid of womanly knowing. Women of my generation were taught, as young women, to shunt aside feelings ... anything of Feminine subjectivity, that is our earth and grounding. It has taken me years to recover from the barrenness of my life ... to finally embrace my truth, rather than to reject it.

"A few months ago, I heard the expression 'A Woman, Distinguishing Her Life,' and I loved the two meanings it had for me ... to graduate or retire with honours, to distinguish herself in that way. But also, to sort and delineate, as I have had to do, so that I could begin to see what really belonged in my life. Distinguishing the content and meaning of my life from everything surrounding it ... allowing the essence of my own individual life, at last, to emerge.

"Towards the end of the summer, late one afternoon, something happened that told me I was finding my thread. One of my women graduate students came by for a conference as she began a new chapter on her thesis. We sat, for a while, towards sunset, discussing her paper and ideas, the caring we both felt for her work.

"Then she read me her first paragraph: 'I am exploring how the Feminine thinking function might differ from the Masculine, how we women might incorporate our consciousness of ourselves as women with our inner Masculine side. It is exciting to consider what might happen in the next few decades if we approach our thinking with a whole new

Feminine awareness: embrace our womanly feeling values as the very warp of our process ... weave between heart and mind to create a whole new wondrous fabric.'

"She put down her thesis and looked at me with tears, 'Thank you for your heart-mind.' "

A fine light breeze rustles the leaves
  against the darkening sky.
    The tiniest star
      sits twinkling on the horizon.

How might your life have been different if, late one afternoon, near the end of the summer, as you thought of the opening of school ... and of trying, again, to learn to use your mind in traditional ways ... something wondrous had happened?

If the women who were your teachers had invited their young women students ... even the littlest girls ... to come to sit in a circle ... and, of course, you went, too.

If you had sensed the excitement in the voices of the teachers as they spoke of a different way to use your fine, young minds. And you could feel the wonder of women sitting in a circle, under the open sky, just outside the school ... gathered to share their wisdom with the younger women in their care.

How might your life be different?

Woman
  sitting on a hillside
    listening . . .
      listening
        as the wind
          . . . blows its eternal questions:

      How can woman
        help her daughters
          enter their inner work?

And the earth

      murmurs her response:

         Enter yourself...

            ...yourself.

HER RETURN
TO FEMININE
GROUND

Her contagion

I sit listening . . .
       the wind blows
            a woman's dream to me:

"I am standing near my house . . . just where the garden is. A group of my women friends have gathered around me. We want to sit down on the ground, but it is covered with a slippery layer of shiny white styrofoam.

"We cannot touch the earth."

As a woman matures, she deepens in her knowledge of her work within . . . moves towards a closer relationship with the Self. By this time, she has worked diligently to find her spiritual direction, struggled to free herself from slavishly following the directives of her Masculine side.

Yet, at this late stage, the Masculine side of the woman exerts a counter-pull: *"Once again, I feel endangered by judgements from my old patriarchs, within as well as without. Now, a subtler form of judgement: after all of my work, why have I not come farther?"*

The animus, not yet won over, is making the last great effort to keep the woman focused on achievements in the outer realm, before she focuses within on the realm of the deeper Self. In response, she must continuously sort herself out so that she can take her stance. For only by her efforts to choose, each time, can she release herself from bondage.

The Masculine side of a woman, at this stage, works with enormous subtlety. *"I suffer a mild contagion, as if I am running a slight fever, that keeps me apart from myself, not available to others. I lose a sense of the realness and substance of my life."* The woman tries to fulfill her tasks in time that does not really exist . . . fills out forms or addresses letters between her daily appointments . . . never allows herself time enough for her freshly washed hair to dry.

The woman's Masculine side still "puts her up to doing something important" without her ever knowing what it should be. It makes her live from outside of herself, flipping back and forth from centeredness to over-dispersed activity . . . unaware of her frenetic ambivalence or of how she betrays herself.

The gravest danger from this contagion is the woman's tendency to be taken over completely by her Masculine side as she is kept from settling into the quiet spaces she has prepared

> . . . she cannot notice
> > the sunlight
> > > drifting in at the window
> > > > . . . the pungence
> > > > > of the scarlet chrysanthemums
> > > > > on her reading table.

Even her daily silences seem stale and contrived.

A group of women sat quietly reflecting on their concerns, troubled by an experience shared the day before. A woman described the incident:

"One woman in our group had spoken at length, giving paragraphs of details that had sounded relevant at first, but had not shared her experience from within the feelings themselves.

"The words seemed to come from her Masculine side instead of from her grounded Feminine ego. She concluded by asking insistently if we understood, as if she sensed how far removed she was from herself."

The woman describing the incident looked distraught: *"As gently as we could, we told her that she had been quite long. But she acted utterly destroyed, claiming hurt beyond measure and huffily insisting that she had thought 'this was a place for sharing.' Still acting from her Masculine side, she accused all of us of being uncaring. Then, in a reaction typical to woman's Masculine side, she stormed away in a bluster. Although we had given our all, it was as nothing to her animus.*

"When our circle gathered the next day, the woman was not with us. We realized sadly that her Masculine side simply might need to run its course. We agreed that we would try to welcome her whenever she returned."

An older woman spoke:

"I feel oppressed when we women are at odds with each other and seem to have so little control over what is happening among us. Of course our inner Masculine side will be active when we enter our silence and our deepest sharing as women! When a woman speaks from her heart and we receive her with ours, all of us are nourished by the true feelings alive in the moment.

"Threatened, the Masculine side of us fears it will lose all of us from its grasp and becomes very active. It begins to

speak, then, with a veneer of sentimentality that invites a moist eye occasionally, but does not allow a woman to weep her deepest tears, which could release us all.

"Our feelings are invalidated . . . the meaning of our lives. We end up quoting old, outer authority, since our own is discounted from within."

The woman paused thoughtfully: *"The most subtly wounding facility is the use of wit. The animus can be mockingly amusing at the expense of a woman's feelings, as a woman dismisses herself or her sister with little jokes and charming stories.*

"I wish there were a way to gently alert a friend when we see her in the grip of that autonomous part of herself . . . a way to stay so grounded that our own Masculine side would not be stirred into action by that side of her. I feel as if I know the signs from painful personal experience.

"I remember a dream in which a grey-cloaked figure welcomed women into a sacred grotto. To my shock, the figure was a man in the robes of an ancient priestess . . . with red high heels showing beneath his hairy leg.

"That was my Masculine side. Had me go into a gathering of women and act omniscient in the very realm of the Feminine where he had no footing at all! Had me holding forth, out-womaning woman in the name of poultice or solstice, simply fulfilling a power drive with no sense of how to be with my sisters as a woman.

"That is the way of the animus! I sometimes think that I can see a woman rise several inches above her chair as that part of her spins her up . . . and keeps all of us from being truly present to her or to ourselves."

As the other women laughed, the woman brushed back her hair.

"And now I'm going to stop myself, for the usual thing is happening . . . I am becoming airy and giddy . . . and I know, by now, that this busy chatter opens the door for my Masculine side. I begin to seek attention. And the next thing that happens is that my Masculine side flings open wide the door and welcomes in all of the negative Feminine in our spitefulness towards each other as women.

"Let me be silent now and find my ground again."

The afternoon sun cast long shadows. One by one, the women entered the silence. The room grew very still. The women parted to rest.

When the women gathered again in the dim light of the evening, the youngest among them broke the silence. Her face, still slender and intense, shone under greying hair:

"I never was able to make a commitment to my life. Three fiancés, three jobs, and a dozen different groups of friends. As a creative child, I received constant attention. I think it was the undeveloped Masculine side of my mother that 'put me up to being special' to make up for what she had not done. Each time I was about to settle down, there was a counter-pull luring me to ever more exciting possibilities.

"I thought I was settling into my life when a situation occurred that brought a needed humility. I had been offered a position of permanence and solidity at a regional center for the arts. The inevitable pattern recurred as the old inner voice asked insinuatingly, 'But won't you be bored with such a provincial audience? What's the harm in staying free?'

"That evening as I struggled with the questions, an image came to me of an old nun who taught mime at the academy many years before, 'Hasn't that inner sorcerer stolen enough from you? What's the harm indeed? Soon he'll steal your life!'

"Her grey eyes stared straight at me: 'It is not enough to come to intellectual awareness of our patterns. We must engage with them and change them, or we deceive ourselves. You have a right to give up the role of the eternally charming girl and ask that your Masculine side give up being an insubstantial boy.' Her grey eyes softened for a moment as they looked straight into mine. 'Claim your dignity and maturity and authority . . . make the choice towards your deepest Self.' "

There was silence to honour the woman's story. An older woman seated near her, nodded in understanding.

"Several years ago, I was invited to read my work in the town where I was born. I selected the material carefully, choosing passages that illustrated women's individuation, our movement away from outer conformity as we become ourselves.

"As the time drew near to return to my birthplace, I found myself frightened and shy . . . tempted to read, not passionately and full-heartedly as was my usual style, but like the schoolgirl those women had known fifty-five years before.

"The day before my journey, I was full of dreadful anxiety. Would I really present my own material in a sterile and 'proper' fashion . . . betray this chance to witness to woman's individuation?

"When I entered the train the next day and tried to settle myself, a comforting image came . . . of a stately and beautiful actress in her role in Ibsen's Ghosts, *which I had seen several seasons before. Her lines rang out, in my memory, of wishing*

77

to live a life of courage and vision, rather than to pass it in servitude to 'dead ideals and worn-out old beliefs.'

"As the waiter served coffee in the dining car, late in the afternoon, I selected the last material for my presentation. For the opening reading, I chose a poem in the voice of a mature woman:

If I am so perpetually terrified
    of being called a bad girl,
so externally blown about
    by the winds of my inner judges,
that I must cling to any authority
    that grants me marginal approval,
then I risk that I might never, ever
    turn towards that within me
that guides and orders my existence,
    that lets the truth of my life emerge.
O! Grant me courage to become myself!"

The wind blows . . . leaves rustle, russet and gold.

How might our lives, as women, be different if there were a place for us to go when we were in dreadful conflict within and at odds with our women friends? ... when we had already struggled with our conflict and couldn't make sense out of it? ... A place where we could be with women more settled than ourselves ... women who had deeply worked with the truth of their own lives?

If we could spill out to those women our confusion and feverishness ... and they would listen quietly and gently, but then point out clearly to us the source of our upset within.

And the honesty and patience of the women ... and knowing that we were heard ... would somehow soothe our pain and allow clarity to emerge.

How might our lives be different?

Her possession

I sit listening . . .
*   the wind blows*
*   a woman's image to me:*

"I had been abducted and was being held captive in a room far above the earth . . . lured there by exquisite praise.

"My captor was a terrifying destroyer of women. If I succumbed to his hypnotizing, I would become a destroyer, too."

As a woman works consciously with the Masculine side of herself, she learns its patterns and behaviours, begins to see, in the moment, how it influences her. Yet, even then, from time to time, she is snatched from behind . . . possessed.

The woman is the last to be aware. Her women friends or her husband are the first to feel the sting . . . and always, her poor children. All that is negative in the Feminine realm floods over the woman at that moment . . . the loathing of herself, neglect and abuse of the elemental . . . her body, family, and household. The door is open to cursing, to the nursing of old hurts, as the woman is taken over by this awesome negative power.

What can help a woman back into herself? Sometimes a woman friend can draw her back into life again by quietly attending her, expressing compassion for her pain. By her loving concern, the friend can help the woman back into relationship with her feelings . . . by her gentle tending, help her back into her body, her simple creaturely needs. The most powerful healing of all will come if the woman can be helped to weep . . . the living emotion in her tears will melt her frozen condition.

If a man tries to intervene, he may be attacked by the woman's rampaging Masculine side. For this side of a woman is only a brittle reflection of the warmth and strength of the true Masculine and will try to destroy the husband and dominate the household.

Only if a man can remember not to be drawn into words, or into competition with the woman's Masculine side, does he stand a chance of bringing her back to her womanly relatedness.

Three women spoke of their anguish when unconsciously possessed by their animus. The first woman described her family life:

"I thought of myself as so spiritual that I was unconscious of my real behaviour. I had no sense that our daily lives were of any importance at all. The house was quite beneath me . . . I would not focus on a task. I didn't care enough for the material realm to bring order to the things of our lives.

"Each morning, my children went out like little disheveled ragamuffins . . . everything all askew. And in the afternoon, when they returned from school, I screamed that they'd interrupted my meditation with their pedestrian concerns. While, to my evening study groups, I presented an opposite image . . . a self-conscious over-centeredness without any freshness or life.

"I blamed it all on my husband, who did not live up to my intellectual or spiritual ideals. He just went to work and came home to his workshop and garden. Thank God that, for the children, he was a warm and encouraging father.

"I don't know what rescued us from that dreadful time in our lives. One day, I found myself thrusting my youngest child away as I prepared to lead my group. I knew something was terribly wrong.

Her tears shocked me out of being possessed by my Masculine side . . . brought me face to face with myself."

There was silence as the three women sensed the full danger in the first woman's experience. The second woman waited . . . then began to speak:

"I carried all of the burdens during those painful years . . . hardened myself against any needs in the Feminine realm.

"I spent those years living totally through the Masculine side of myself . . . Hardening my heart for so long let something else slip in the door. I can see it in the photographs taken of me during that time . . . the set of my jaw, the tilt of my head . . . my face became tough and cold.

"When I look back, at myself, it is with a deep compassion. I needed to have that toughness, then, but also to let it go. How impatient that harder side of me was with my womanly needs and hurt. I could not face the pain underneath or minister to it myself.

"Saddest of all was the loneliness. Women friends were driven away by my competitiveness, except for a very few who were as possessed as I. But I could not bear their cutoffness from feelings any more than they could bear mine. One by one, they all left.

"Isolated and alone, I spent those terrible years hating men, most women, and, of course, myself. What finally broke the alienation was being held by a warm, silent man who refused to be drawn into words . . . simply held me closely until I started to cry. As my weeping deepened into sobs, I began to return to myself."

The three women sat in silence, to honour the woman's words . . . parted quietly to prepare a cup of tea.

When the women came together again, they gathered close around the fire. The third woman began to speak:

"I was touched as you spoke of being silently held and returning to yourself. My experience was quite different. I was full of anger at my husband. He had said something that hurt me, and I held it to my heart.

"What could have been useful anger, if I had communicated it, became an entrenched rage. The insult became precious and exaggerated as I nursed my grievances and refused my husband's apologies.

"I can see, now, the Masculine posturing in what I did and how it cut me off from my husband's caring and honest concern. Even as my husband apologized, my animus convinced me that I was right, and I shoved my husband away. If only I had been able to let the flesh-and-blood man reach me, the inner impostor would have been exposed.

"One morning, I realized that I couldn't stop being nasty to my husband. I felt as miserable as he. Yet, I was caught in something perverse that wouldn't let loose of either of us.

"Late that afternoon, a woman friend dropped by and took me briefly aside. She spoke with me quietly and caringly . . . seemed to see my pain. Rather than drawing me into words, she simply reached out her hand . . . she stroked my aching head. She must have known how desperately I had needed to cry . . . for I sobbed a long while after she wrapped my shoulders warmly in her sweater.

"She asked if I would come with her the next day for the baths and massage, then gently spoke to my husband so that somehow he understood.

"In the few days after that, the woman came back several times. We scrubbed with a bucket of hot suds . . . the whole house, the walls, the floors. Then, as the last rays of the late afternoon sun bathed the room, we washed the windows in my study.

"Through a familiar and comforting task, she brought me back to the realm of matter, to my body and my household . . . back to my Feminine ego.

"The warmth of the water in the bucket seemed to melt what was so frozen. Life could flow again."

The wind blows lightly . . . leaves drift down.

How might it have been different for you, when you were terribly upset and full of harsh self-judgement, if there had been a place where you would be received by a woman whom you trusted?

If the woman had listened in silence as you began to speak? And there had been a feeling of such simple acceptance that you were able to weep... finally, able to weep out all of the confusion and pain that you had held inside for so long.

How might your life be different?

Her individuation

I sit listening . . .
    The wind blows
        a woman's image to me:

"Although the schedule had been pressing, I felt quite satisfied at a recent decision to take more time for myself . . . one-half hour a day, for walking or reflection.

"Then, that night, I awoke and was transfixed by moonlight streaming in at the window . . . and at the image of a woman . . . scrawny and malnourished . . . her face covered with ashes . . . clothing torn by thorns.

"'I am the neglected and crazy part of you . . . the holy part inside, which you so often deny . . . bustling between kitchen and studio, cheerful and productive.

" 'Don't you see I am dying?

    When will you recognize me
        as the most precious part of yourself?

        When will you grant me sovereignty?

        When will you give me your soul?'

"I knelt and wept in the moonlight . . .
    . . . let my tears wash the ashes from her face."

The years pass. A woman matures. Her work with her Masculine side ripens . . . her contributions to the society around her carefully brought to harvest. The Self calls insistently. She must finally hear and respond . . . or take the other path of hardening her heart against the voice within calling her to become herself.

A woman must be very clear, here, in her ongoing task. As she negotiates the voyage from the societal towards the Self, her entire experience is transformed. She can begin to reject the inner patriarchal decrees from the past that judged her so mercilessly . . . that made her see her own anguish as simply another indication of her inadequacy and shame.

With this transformation, a woman can accept feelings inside herself that were forbidden to her before. She can accept, newly, her failures, her lacks, her obsessions . . . even her occasional craziness . . . as she holds in her awareness all the ways she has suffered in striving to fulfill values that were not her own.

At last a woman cradles in her arms the woundedness of being herself. No longer casting it out as the impediment that prevents her growth, she can embrace her woundedness as the essence, the soul of her uniqueness . . . that which has enabled her to become herself.

With this final acceptance of her woundedness, a woman's perception of her own suffering undergoes a profound healing. What had been the source of greatest shame, that most loathed in herself, slowly reveals itself to her as the seed of her truest gift . . . her pearl of greatest price, grown from her gravest flaw. She is released into her wholeness.

Finally, as a woman matures, she gives up the expectation of reaching a point of bare adequacy and moving on from there. At last, she understands that her task is simply to accept her woundedness ... and to walk ahead with courage and compassion ... keeping faith with her own life.

This is her individuation.

A woman sat alone and considered her condition. She was an editor of scientific journals who had recovered from starvation in all aspects of her life:

"I began to feel the poignancy of my own wounding ... the poignancy of those old patterns set up, so long ago, as a protection against further wounding, in my little child way.

"I said, once, to my counsellor many months ago, 'But my patterns are pathological,' and she replied, 'Then that is finally what makes all the going back into one's personal history worthwhile. To be able to see the original wounding with such pathos, that you at last can feel compassion for that terribly wounded little child who wanted so strongly to survive that she was willing to adopt extreme patterns.'

"From the moment I heard those words, I knew that I must trust that my uniqueness stemmed from my own kind of wounding ... grew directly out of it, not divorced or split off from it. I knew, from that day forward, that one day I would be able to stop loathing my woundedness ... and hold it in esteem."

A second woman spoke:

"I couldn't imagine taking the risk of becoming more myself. All I had ever experienced was humiliation and despair for revealing, in any way, who I really was. My parents must have wanted a completely different child! Any way in which I was gifted was not enough for them. If my talents could not win instant fame, I was scorned for even trying.

"My animus reflected the negating attitude of my parents. Years ago, I named my inner negating figures 'the shit boys.' Far from being helpers who supported my efforts to develop, they were the eternal critics who scorned anything I brought forth from within myself.

"I learned quite skillfully, over the years, to submerge my own feelings and needs . . . to use myself as mirror and mentor for the creativity of others. I could help bring out their spirit, while mine was held captive within.

"I have helped many wordless people express themselves in poems . . . helped those with no sense of identity tell the pathos of their lives as they wrote autobiographies. I have watched the radiance of dance emerge from eighty- and ninety-year-old bodies as our troupe toured the countryside working with the elderly.

"I have had to realize, as my deepest truth, that I could help bring another's gift to life, but that my own wounding is so severe that it is still terrifyingly dangerous for me to consider living as myself.

"I wish, now, to be present to what is real within . . . to the anguish and chaos and fear . . . no longer to dress it up in impeccable tutorial service to the creativity of others. In the past, I fooled myself, because I managed to do that so

well . . . further and further estranged from myself . . . feeding on anything to fill the hollow.

"There are poems unborn inside me, and, if I live long enough, I wish to bring them to birth, if I can stand against the constant expectation of disgrace for daring to have something inside of me of my very own.

"I know that it is important that I stay close to my apprehension of being immediately shamed. For if I only rise above my fear, as I have so often done, there will be no one to witness my wretchedness and mortification . . . no one to attend my wounding . . . no one to allow it to begin its process of transformation and healing.

"I have finally acknowledged my wounding as the thing in all the world that is most truly mine . . . and that acknowledgement has allowed me to begin to be myself.

"I am able, at last, to witness my wounding . . . and I am, at last, in peace."

The sky darkens towards the evening.

How might your life have been different if, once as you sat in the darkness, suffering the most piercing shame for simply being yourself . . . you had sensed a presence nearby, sitting quietly in the shadows attending you . . . a forgiving Feminine presence?

If you had felt such a flow of compassion from that ancient presence . . . that you could begin to accept your flaws, even your gravest faults? And deeply comforted in the flow of that compassion, you were able, at last, to embrace your own woundedness.

How might your life be different?

Her return

I sit listening . . .
  The wind blows
    a woman's image to me:

"I have crossed a chasm . . . stand alone, now, in a chamber . . . carved of dark, rich crystals, glowing deep within the earth.

"A distant call beckons me onward . . . to a still more glowing chamber . . . then to another, richer still . . . chamber opening unto chamber, each glows more darkly than the last.

"I know that these are the chambers of a mansion that once belonged to my Mother . . .

"And I know that the openings . . .
  chamber unto chamber . . .
    are the moments of my life."

Out of a woman's acceptance of her woundedness comes a quietness and sense of peace. The transformation of the Masculine energy within her from negating to supporting allows her to become herself. She redirects her efforts from the outer to the inner realm . . . finally makes the return to Archetypal Feminine ground with her roots in the guiding principles of the deeper Self.

A woman speaks:

"I feel as if I am becoming who I was meant to be. After all the years of outer-directed energy, I am coming home to the Feminine . . . coming home to myself. I am allowing myself to become a mature woman in the truest and deepest sense.

"Sometimes, as I sit listening quietly within, it seems as if the very air in the house has been transformed . . . a hush of tranquillity, an attitude of devotion filling every room.

"I feel a sense of connection to the self that I have been at other times in my life . . . to the girl and maiden from the past, to the developed woman of adulthood . . . and to the older woman I know that I shall someday be.

"As I allow myself to mature, a clarity emerges, never there before. I seem to know more surely than I have ever known what is mine to do, what must be left undone. There is a growing strength within me . . . and I realize that, while life's difficulties do not disappear, my steadfastness holds firm.

"As I allow myself to mature, an awareness comes of a slender ribbon of energy, no longer robust, as in my youth. I learn to tend it carefully . . . avoid excess, exercise restraint. To use my strength ever more sacramentally, for I suffer more each time I use it in service to old distractions.

"As I allow myself to mature, I find that I must do things the old, slow ways . . . perform my work so quietly that some part of me can always be listening . . . listening for the deeper sense of my life. Those few brief moments each day, that 'closet' in time that, as a young woman, I set aside for myself to listen, are no longer enough for me.

"What I could slip by with while I was still in service to the values of the society around me is likely to make me ill at the level of the Self. I sense that the greater quantity of my time is being required, now, to reflect at the window seat . . . to see the leaves drift down . . . watch the snow clouds gather.

"As I allow myself to mature, I see that if I depart from my center and am over-busy for too long, it may take many days of quietness for me to make the return. And in dry periods, when the Self seems not to be present, I know that my task is simply to wait. Now, the only task . . . in devotion and submission . . . is to wait upon the Self."

Slowly over the years, as a woman allows herself to mature, she sees that she must keep the physical realm so simple that each object in her household becomes translucent . . . revealing its meaning and spirit to her as she polishes it in her hands . . . that this is her testament of devotion, the loving redirection of her energy from outer to inner realm . . . and the holding and hallowing in her hands of the moments of life itself.

Alone on the barren rocks,
I listen to the wind . . .
It blows the ancient, raucous call
of distant wild geese.
I know I am coming home.

How might your life have been different if, through the years, you had felt that there would finally be time enough for you?

If, very early one morning . . . as you sat at the window seat and watched a silvery mist slowly rise from the meadow . . . you heard, far off in the distance, the cry of the wild geese?

And you remembered the first time you had heard that cry, many years before . . . with a chill up the back of your neck? And that you had known, even then, that the haunting, primordial cry . . . was the call of the ancient Feminine returning?

How might your life be different?

Her legacy

I sit listening . . .
        the wind blows
                a child's song to me:

"This is the way we wash our clothes
                        wash our clothes
                                wash our clothes
        this is the way we wash our clothes
                        so early Monday morning.
        This is the way we mend our clothes
                        so early Tuesday morning . . . "

An old woman sits in the dusk, an unlighted candle on the table before her. She picks up a soft cloth, begins to polish the small statue in her hands, as she has done many times before. She polishes the statue of a woman . . . keeping vigil in the stillness . . . polishing her own sense of life.

She hums a children's song that she says is very old . . . then she begins to sing:

" 'This is the way we sow our seed . . .
                        gather our grain . . .
                                bake our bread . . .
        This is the way we tend our lives
                        so early in the morning.'

"I learned that song, and others like it, at an afternoon gathering for children and their mothers, many years ago. Songs that told of the ways of woman, long before I was born . . . still knowing that the spirit with which a task was fulfilled made a difference in the greater order . . . and let a rhythm and meaning emerge from every step of her work.

"Woman, long ago, still in touch with the mysteries of nature . . . singing to the grass and the wind . . . knowing that her song was heard. Pouring out her devotion, as she poured out her menstrual blood, back to the earth again."

The old woman sighs: *"Ah, those young mothers, that afternoon, had lost touch with so much of that. I cannot forget their faces, so desperate and stricken, as they sang their choruses of the ancient circle dances there in the meadow with their children, cut off from any meaning that might have made their tasks alive.*

"That generation of woman, cut off from roots in the earth, or from knowing how to replenish the earth with their own womanly flow . . . so much of their Feminine energies blocked within them, like their milk, in those decades when women heeded the advice to schedule and bottle-feed their young.

"I sang a lament, that afternoon in the meadow, for women of every age, overburdened and overworked . . . a lament that a young woman's inner work had to be accomplished in time that did not exist . . . pressed between efforts for those she loved and the weight of her work in the world.

"I sang a lament for the suffering I saw in the faces of the women who no longer knew how to let their own lives be alive and lead them. I mourned the death of Kairos . . . grieved that a patriarchal ordering so pervaded that women

no longer encouraged in each other an opening unto each moment that could allow it to unfold to the next."

The old woman pushes a strand of hair from her face: "Ah, that was so long ago . . . so many ways were lost. I learned the songs as well as I could, so that someone might keep them alive.

"Once, as our circle of women came together a few years ago, I wakened, restless in the night . . . unable to go back to sleep. I sat for a long time on the terrace, wrapped in a woolen robe . . . watching the moon shine down on the wind-bared trees below.

"When I finally came back to the cottage, there was a glimmer of light from the kitchen. My old friend sat there, alone, by candlelight, the only one in the circle older than I. She polished this little statue that night, telling me of her life . . . and mine.

"She left me her shawl when she died.

"She's gone now, but every year at this season, in the middle of the night, I sit, as she did, for so many years, polishing this statue . . . polishing, alone, while the younger women sleep."

The old woman puts down the statue, reaches for the matches to light the candle:

"That afternoon, long ago, I lamented. But as I sit polishing this statue, I know that a difference can be made as we women remember again to keep faith with our ancient ground.

"We lost touch, in the busyness of this world, with how a difference can be made as we sit in the glow of a candle . . . that the stillness at our center can spread in circles around us, help return a quiet order to the cosmos reflecting us.

"We lost touch for a little while, but I know that a difference can be made if we women can remember that our blood and passion are needed . . . our fierce, tender love for the land. We can bring the cycle to wholeness again as we pour out our devotion . . . as we sing, once more, to the earth."

The old woman unfolds the shawl, wraps it around herself.

"We lost touch for a little while, in the noise and pain around us. But, I know that, for the children, a difference can be made if we can return to a sense of the ancient Maternal . . . return to the cradling embrace that offers solace and protection . . . that strengthens their sense of Self.

"We lost touch for a little while, but I know that, for the men around us, a difference can be made if we can remember a way of being that gives them a place to return, a Yin to receive their Yang warmth. A difference can be made as we help them learn to heal their own pain as well as ours . . . help them comfort their fears and affirm their heroic strivings."

The old woman smoothes the shawl . . . straightens her shoulders beneath it.

"The earth, the children, the men, all needed what was lost. But it is for our daughters . . . our daughters . . . that women must remember all that was left behind. It is our daughters who cannot go on with their lives unless we show them the way.

"It is for our daughters that we must rekindle the ancient ways of the Yin ... help them hold the truth of their knowing deep within themselves and witness it with the full passion and power of their womanly being ... help them remember that the truth each woman holds within will come to realization not only through outer doing but through her inner holding.

"We lost touch for a little while, as we gained power over things seen, that woman's ancient chthonic power has to do with things unseen. For our daughters, we must return to the sacred Feminine ways of holding within our hearts our visions for their lives ...

> *Of holding within,*
> *the essence and splendor*
> *of our daughters' possibilities ...*
> *... the possibilities of all women*
> *... and dreaming them into being."*

The old woman quietly picks up the statue and bends her head low to her task. As the candle flickers out, she sits in the darkness

> *... polishing*
> *... polishing.*

How might your life have been different if, one morning in the earliest springtime, something had drawn you to the woods? And in the cool mist, you had seen women of all ages, from every epoch in history, waiting in the stillness.

And you had knelt among them ... had heard the trembling in the voices of the older women as they spoke of preparation, of individual sacrifice ... of woman offering out of her own uniqueness, her suffering, her devotion. And if, as you listened, you had a glimmer of hope that your work to develop yourself might make a tiny difference ... help heal an ancient Archetype ... restore a longed-for balance in the greater cosmos.

And you felt a sense of wonder, knowing that each woman kneeling there was considering inside herself what her offering would be.

How might your life be different?

Woman
        sitting on a hillside
            listening . . .
                listening
                    as the wind
                        . . . blows its eternal questions:

                    How can woman
                        help her daughters
                            know the Feminine Self?

And the earth
whispers her response:

Know yourself...
...yourself.

The Author

Judith Duerk

Born in the Midwest of a family with strong religious ties, Judith Duerk followed the call of her early love for music. She earned B.S. and M.S. degrees from The Juilliard School, studied as a postgraduate at the Mozarteum in Salzburg and at Indiana University, and taught music at the university level before beginning preparatory work in the field of psychotherapy.

For many years, she has led groups of women on Retreat. She says, "I am awed by the depth of healing that comes as women sit in a circle, by the power of women keeping silence together, and by the truth in their sharing." In addition to her daily work as psychotherapist, she teaches T'ai Chi Ch'uan and works with the ancient Taoist healing art of Chi Kung.

Judith notes that the sensitivity and spiritual strength of the men around her have been helpful role models for her animus. Her two sons are grown. Her husband is a woodsman and hunter. Their lives have been deeply nurtured by the greater cycles of nature, and they seek to know how to nurture those cycles in return.

Other LuraMedia Publications

BANKSON, MARJORY ZOET

Braided Streams:
Esther and a Woman's Way of Growing

Seasons of Friendship:
Naomi and Ruth as a Pattern

"This Is My Body. . .":
Creativity, Clay, and Change

BOHLER, CAROLYN STAHL

Prayer on Wings: *A Search for Authentic Prayer*

DOHERTY, DOROTHY ALBRACHT
and McNAMARA, MARY COLGAN

Out of the Skin Into the Soul:
The Art of Aging

GEIGER, LURA JANE
and PATRICIA BACKMAN
Braided Streams Leader's Guide
and SUSAN TOBIAS
Seasons of Friendship Leader's Guide

GOODSON, WILLIAMSON (with Dale J.)
Re-Souled: *Spiritual Awakenings of a Psychiatrist and His Patient in Alcohol Recovery*

JEVNE, RONNA FAY

It All Begins With Hope:
Patients, Caretakers, and the Bereaved Speak Out

and ALEXANDER LEVITAN

No Time for Nonsense:
Getting Well Against the Odds

KEIFFER, ANN

Gift of the Dark Angel: *A Woman's Journey through Depression toward Wholeness*

LODER, TED

Eavesdropping on the Echoes:
Voices from the Old Testament

Guerrillas of Grace:
Prayers for the Battle

Tracks in the Straw:
Tales Spun from the Manger

Wrestling the Light:
Ache and Awe in the Human-Divine Struggle

MEYER, RICHARD C.

One Anothering:
Biblical Building Blocks for Small Groups

MILLETT, CRAIG

In God's Image:
Archetypes of Women in Scripture

PRICE, H.H.

Blackberry Season:
A Time to Mourn, A Time to Heal

RAFFA, JEAN BENEDICT

The Bridge to Wholeness:
A Feminine Alternative to the Hero Myth

Dream Theatres of the Soul:
Empowering the Feminine through Jungian Dreamwork

SAURO, JOAN

Whole Earth Meditation:
Ecology for the Spirit

SCHAPER, DONNA

Stripping Down:
The Art of Spiritual Restoration

WEEMS, RENITA J.

Just a Sister Away: *A Womanist Vision of Women's Relationships in the Bible*

I Asked for Intimacy: *Stories of Blessings, Betrayals, and Birthings*

The Women's Series

BORTON, JOAN

Drawing from the Women's Well:
Reflections on the Life Passage of Menopause

CARTLEDGE-HAYES, MARY

To Love Delilah:
Claiming the Women of the Bible

DUERK, JUDITH

Circle of Stones:
Woman's Journey to Herself

I Sit Listening to the Wind:
Woman's Encounter within Herself

O'HALLORAN, SUSAN and
DELATTRE, SUSAN

The Woman Who Lost Her Heart:
A Tale of Reawakening

RUPP, JOYCE

The Star in My Heart:
Experiencing Sophia, Inner Wisdom

SCHNEIDER-AKER, KATHERINE

God's Forgotten Daughter:
A Modern Midrash: What If Jesus Had Been A Woman?

LuraMedia, Inc. , 7060 Miramar Rd., Suite 104, San Diego, CA 92121
Call 1-800-FOR-LURA for information about bookstores or ordering.
Books for Healing and Hope, Balance and Justice.